A Whiting & Birch Ltd / SCA Co-Publication

Linkages:

effective networking in social care

Malcolm Payne

Whiting and Birch Ltd

1993

Published by Whiting & Birch Ltd, PO Box 872, Forest Hill, London SE23 3HL, England.
USA: Paul & Co, Publishers' Consortium Inc, PO Box 442, Concord, MA 017422.

British Library Cataloguing in Publication Data.
A CIP catalogue record ins available from the British Library

ISBN 1 871177 50 2 (cased)
ISBN 1 871177 34 0 (limp)

Printed in England by Bourne Press, Poole

Contents

FOREWORD AND ACKNOWLEDGEMENTS ix

1: INTRODUCTION 1
The importance of linkages
Elements of linking
Aims and organisation of the book

2: PLANNING AND MANAGING LINKING 8
Management decisions about linking
Aims and priorities
Table 1 Linkage aims in a local Age Concern group
Methods
*Table 2 Methods of linking used by a social services area team
with its local social security office*
Timescale
Resources
Conclusion
Exercises - Chapter 2
1 Assessing links
2 Assessing the aims of links
3 Identifying the methods of linking in use
4 Identifying timescale and resource limitations and
   requirements

3: LIAISON 18
What is liaison?
The liaison process
Liaison systems
Planning liaison
Exercises - Chapter 3
1 Checking liaison arrangements and aims
2 Liaison processes
3 Liaison systems

4: FIRST APPROACHES 24
First approaches are important
The right person
The right image

The right subject
The right resources
Exercises - Chapter 4
1 Assessing an organisation for the right approach
2 Reviewing the approachability of you or your own organisation
3 Looking at yourself
4 Difficult situations

5: LINKING STYLES 32
Personal style and approach
Patterns and structures
Setting and medium
Intrusion and involvement
Conflict and confrontation
Conclusion
Exercises - Chapter 5
1 Assessing personal style
2 Evaluating style in practice
3 Assessing pattern and structure
4 Dealing with conflict/confrontation

6: PREPARATION AND TRAINING FOR LINKING WORK.... 40
The need for preparation and training
Preparation
Training
Examples of preparation
Handing over
Exercises - Chapter 6
1 Working on a training programme for linkers on behalf of an organisation
2 Working on a training programme for linkers in an individual case
3 Planning an handover strategy

7: WHEN THINGS GO WRONG 47
Prevention
Confrontation
Mistakes and disasters
Dealing with complaints
Exercises - Chapter 7
1 Identifying misinterpretation
2 Practising misinterpretation (for a team)
3 Confrontations
4 Likely complaints
5 Complaints system

8: CO-ORDINATION 55
Moving on to structured linking through co-ordination
Avoiding gaps
Avoiding overlaps

Aligned strategies
Developing aligned attitudes and values
Integrated structures
Conclusion
Exercises - Chapter 8
1 Considering needs for co-ordination
2 Planning co-ordination
3 Approaching co-ordination

9: ADVOCACY, ALLIANCE AND COALITION 66
The importance of creating alliances
The role of advocacy
Building alliances
Conclusion
Exercises - Chapter 9
1 Assessing support
2 Planning an alliance

10: REPRESENTATIVE ROLES 74
Understanding representative roles
Four common representative roles
Conclusion
Exercise - Chapter 10
Assessing linking roles

11: BEING EFFECTIVE IN COMMITTEE 81
Committee work is important
Committee procedure
Committee members' responsibilities
Conclusion
Exercises - Chapter 11
1 Reviewing committee membership
2 Practising committee work
3 Raising difficult issues

12: COMMITTEE AND MEETINGS STRATEGY 92
Why you need a strategy
Watching brief
Disinterested commentator
Respondent
Active involvement
Directed involvement
Leadership
Conclusion
Exercises - Chapter 12
1 Evaluating committee strategy
2 Practising committee strategy

13: REPORTING BACK 99
The importance of reporting back

Methods of reporting back
Meetings: an example of reporting back processes
Conclusion
Exercises - Chapter 13
1 Reviewing reporting back arrangements
2 Reporting back techniques

14: LOBBYING 104
What is lobbying?
Lobbying locations
Means of Influence
The lobbying process
Conclusion
Exercises - Chapter 14
1 Assessing lobbying needs and opportunities
2 Assessing your vulnerability

15: FORMAL PRESENTATIONS 110
The problems of presenting your organisation or needs
Public presentations
Structures for speaking
Making presentations
Public address systems
Dealing with reporters
Radio and television
Exhibitions
Publications
Conclusion
Exercises - Chapter 15
1 Strategies for formal presentations
2 Practising formal presentations

BIBLIOGRAPHY 123

Foreword &

Acknowledgements

This book originally started as a shorter and more informal text for voluntary organisations and their members. I am grateful to Patrick Wright for encouraging me to write it and to Susan Clayton for reading and commenting on drafts. When this came to nothing, due to my passing on to other activities and the exigencies of voluntary sector publishing, I retained my interest in the topics covered and have re-written the original with more general purposes in mind, for the reasons and with the aims set out in the Introduction (Chapter 1).

However, I hope it retains much of its informality and practical value. Some people may question the more elementary matters covered here and say that students and workers in the social and community services will have moved beyond these. I am afraid that this is not my experience. Many of them are unconfident and unwilling in making links with other organisations. I feel, therefore, a fairly practical guide is valuable for many practitioners in the social and community services and students working towards qualifications in that field.

Nonetheless, I have also built up the sections of the book which consider basic principles and ideas such as intrusion which I think are crucial in understanding what you are doing and applying that understanding to a wide range of linking work. So this version of *Linkages* aims to satisfy the need for a fairly practical guide within a context of ideas about the practice. Its practical emphasis does mean that I have avoided all but minimal references to books and articles, but there is a list of further reading at the end which I hope will be useful.

Malcolm Payne
Didsbury, 1993

One: introduction

THE IMPORTANCE OF LINKAGES

This book is about making links between community and voluntary organisations through personal contacts and relationships. It also applies to the increasing number of private social care organisations which must build and sustain relationships with other related organisations. It aims to help social workers and other people working in social and health care and community affairs, no matter what setting they work in, and committee members and voluntary workers make sense of the task of keeping in touch with related services.

Making and maintaining links between organisations and between individuals involved in caring and the organisations that might help (or hinder) them is a vital part of social care. Most definitions of social work tasks include activities such as liaison, mobilising resources, negotiating and advocacy on behalf of the people that social workers serve.

Most caring tasks should not be done alone; they usually involve several agencies and helpers. This is because much caring is onerous, and those involved need support and a feeling that others value and participate in what they do. Caring is also complex; it involves many different skills, and most people do not possess them all. For the relative or friend either just helping out or dedicating their life to caring responsibilities this can be a pressure. They may be forced to take on things that they do not like doing, or cannot do well. For the professional, their strengths and training may limit the contribution they can make, and in difficult circumstances they may need to call on the skills and training of someone with a different training and expertise.

In all of these instances, and in many more, we need to call on the involvement of others, and organise what they do so that it works best for the person we are trying to help. Where this involves connecting up organised services with more informal provision, this is called *interweaving*, a term invented by Michael Bayley (1973). Interweaving implies that what we are about is making the services work together as a seamless piece of cloth, in which everything relates to other aspects of the service to make a pattern which works best for the person being served.

The reasons for building up linkages include aspects of service which are not aimed at personal help. Among the important facets of social work is social action and social development. We are always concerned to improve services, and to involve people who receive the services, their supporters and the community around them in those developments. A crucial aspect of doing so is creating organisations and alliances between them that will gain support and foster the improvements that we wish to see. Experience of achieving such improvements can be a powerful and valuable experience for many people who are oppressed either by the personal lives which throw such a burden of demands upon them, or by systematic oppression which is inherent in the ways that our society has structured into it inequalities and injustices in relationships between human beings and social groups. These oppressions have been particularly apparent to people working in community, social and health care, as they have come to understand the disadvantage built into the lives of many people from ethnic minorities, many women and disabled people. Oppression is often strengthened by class and other social divisions.

This sort of work has been the preserve of community workers, and many social workers and people from similar professions have felt that they have no expertise or interest in furthering it. Many people, coming to local social affairs or needing to use the network of community and social care organisations for the first time, have been bemused and disabled from involvement by the complexity and difficulty of gaining any impact on the problem they want to solve.

In the 1990s, however, getting involved in the network of social and community care is not an option for many of us - it is a necessity. The demand for long-term care is growing, since there is a higher proportion of elderly people in the population, and government policy, medical advances and people's wishes mean that more people with major disabilities, either physical, mental or both, will be living outside institutions. Family and social relationships are changing, so that family care is less available, or less strong than it once was. This means that interweaving family, informal and more organised care is becoming more and more important. We are all likely to have to do more caring in our private lives than we expected at the height of welfare state provision, although we may do no more than our parents in their generation (see Bulmer, 1987).

Government policy in the 1980s, particularly the development of community care policy towards the end of that period, led to increasing importance being given to the skills of making links. So also did the 1980s development of 'community social work' in the UK. These two developments in policy thinking form an essential background to the work of professionals in the social and health services. They also show the trends that all carers, whether they act as individuals or as professionals, will have to cope with in the 1990s.

The Griffiths Report (1988) on *community care* and the policy and services changes resulting from it (particularly the National Health Service and Community Care Act 1990) and related policy developments have led to greater importance being given to building up 'packages of care' for individual people which meet their unique needs, instead of providing set services, which may only partially meet needs. Services will not be provided by a few large official agencies, but instead by a myriad of smaller private, voluntary and informal groups. This places a premium on helping people through a much more complex system of caring, and finding pathways to the help which is relevant for them.

Case management, a technique pioneered in the UK by the Kent Community Care scheme (Davies and Challis, 1986), aims to promote this form of individualised care. Among the main elements of case management are: developing a range of alternative services which can be called into play for particular people; using the network of services and contacts in a community to identify people in need; negotiating and bringing together services in a package that works; following up the way in which services work together; and adapting this work as services, needs and preferences change and checking and evaluating how the services work together. All this obviously makes developing the skills of working together with informal carers and other services a more central part of social work than it is with many conventional casework services.

Community social work is a way of organising the work of social services teams so that a small group of professionally qualified workers share responsibility for a small geographical area with a group of ancillary workers, such as home helps, social work assistants and occupational therapists (Hadley and

McGrath, 1984). The teams involve themselves more closely in the community than is the case with conventional social work, thus learning about problems before they become serious, and stimulating informal, collective and community efforts at responding to problems, whether individual or more widespread. Again, this implies a concern for greater efforts to be made to foster community links from professionals and among local organisations and individuals (see Hadley *et al.*, 1984; Domoney, 1989).

Similar developments, all using these skills, may be seen in the development of community mental handicap teams, involving several different professionals, clients and patients and informal carers and community organisations in planning for people with mental handicaps (Grant *et al.*, 1987). The term now used for such conditions is people with 'learning difficulties' which emphasises the possibilities of overcoming difficulty rather than the assumption, which often goes with the word 'handicap', that it is something which must be lived with.

Other professions working in the community have also begun to develop linking skills, for example community psychiatric nurses, as with the growth of community care this professional group develops its work outside hospitals. People working with voluntary organisations have always needed to use the skills of making and sustaining contacts with parts of the network of services within which their group exists.

ELEMENTS OF LINKING

Making and maintaining links involves a range of skills which are related to one another. These may be divided into four main groups, which are dealt with successively in this book:

- *liaison* which is about making contact with other organisations and sustaining that contact;
- *co-ordination* which is about ensuring that the organisations work together when this is necessary; generally this relies on liaison skills;
- *representation* which is about acting on behalf of your agency, organisation or client with another agency or person;
- *presentation* which is about promoting and demonstrating the value and work of your organisation, so that people may understand and use it better.

Each of these has connections with other aspects of work in the community. They are all related to management; self-management of individual workers, management of the work that has to be done, and the management of the organisation. This is because linking involves consistency and planning if it is to work well. Also, since it involves more than one organisation or grouping of individuals, linking usually forces the people involved in the activity to create policy, about themselves and their organisation and about others. This arises because you have to define yourselves and what you are about in dealing with the other organisation; it also means that you have to have an understanding of the other organisation. A good deal of such policy is covert. Explicit policies about how to deal with the other organisation are rare, but I argue that you will always have some views which are implicit, and that there is often benefit to be gained in understanding clearly and planning for your linking work. Linking policy may need to be at individual, team or organisational levels.

Linking work is also related to public relations and publicity work; in many ways representation and presentation skills develop directly into public relations. However, this book is concerned with personal linking, rather than collective representation and the emphasis here is on the skills involved in making contact personally, rather than through campaigns and publications.

Similarly, linking connects with advocacy (both for individuals and causes) and community, political and social action. In the 1980s a movement for promoting advocacy on behalf of people with handicap and disadvantage has grown up. This built on a tradition of advocacy on behalf of individuals where their cases were inadequately dealt with by the state or other services, and on behalf of causes, where there was collective injustice. More recently, there has grown a movement for citizen advocacy on behalf of groups of disadvantaged people, involving their own development of skills in self-advocacy with mutual support between them (Butler *et al.*, 1988). But although some of the skills are relevant and shared, and people involved in such work may therefore find it useful, the main focus of this book is day-to-day practice in social service and similar organisations, and help for individuals dealing with and relating to such services.

Many linking skills are also relevant for development work, in trying to establish new services or improve existing ones. Again, however, I stop short of considering project planning and development work, which is more of a managerial task, although other workers do get involved in such work from time to time.

To sum up the skills involved in linking work, they are:

- careful planning and strategy;
- thinking about and using different settings;
- effective use of interpersonal skills

AIMS AND ORGANISATION OF THE BOOK

The aims that I have in writing this book are as follows:

- to assert and demonstrate the importance of linking work in social work and related activities in the community;
- to analyse and describe the skills involved in linking work;
- to help workers in social and other related services develop skills in linking work;
- to describe and promote effective planning of linking work.

The book is set out in a series of short chapters. Chapters 1 and 2 form a general introduction, offer some basic principles, and suggest ways of planning and managing linking work, including dealing with some of the problems. Following this, Chapters 3-7 are concerned with liaison in its various aspects, including preparation and training, Chapters 8 and 9 with co-ordination, Chapters 10-13 with representation and Chapters 14 and 15 with presentation. Each chapter contains some explanatory material which aims to help you understand and analyse what you are doing; and, where appropriate, practical advice and information, and exercises to enable you to practise and plan work in the area covered.

The aim of the book is to provide a practice guide. It is written in a way which assumes that you may be using the information personally to improve your work, and so most of the exercises relate to an individual reader. However, it is a basic principle of mine that much of this work is best done co-operatively by a team of people working on issues together, and most things can be adapted to a team developing linking work as a project or as part of wider activities.

Throughout the book, I have written as though I am addressing a person in one organisation (which I have therefore called 'your organisation' or 'your own organisation') who is linking with another organisation (which I sometimes call the 'host' or 'target' organisation because it acts as a host to your representative or because you aim to influence or link with it). If necessary, you need to interpret 'you' and 'your' to refer to your team, or a group of people working together. You may find some of this terminology irritating because 'host' emphasises the aspect of representation which intrudes on an organisation (see Chapter 5 for a further discussion of the concept of 'intrusion') and 'target' implies a rather aggressive managerial approach to the issue. But being able to specify which organisation I am referring to is sometimes useful for clarity and I hope you will compensate for any inappropriate nuances as you go along.

Another important reminder: while I discuss mainly work with an 'outside' organisation as the host, if you work in one part of a large organisation such as a social services department or health authority, your 'target' may be another part of or grouping in the same organisation.

I have written this book for three main reasons. The first is that I think this aspect of social work is very important and rather neglected, so it needs the emphasis of a book to itself.

The second is that it develops from two previous books (Payne, 1982; 1986) which cover some of these issues. I have been dissatisfied with the amount of attention I was able to give the subject in those books, and I wanted to draw together material which is quite scattered in those books and my other writings. I think this is a topic which should be seen and pulled together.

The third reason for writing this book is that it is a topic that interests and stimulates me. I have spent more than twenty years working with voluntary and community organisations, and trying to link them with official agencies, as a social worker, manager, volunteer and latterly as an employee of voluntary organisations, both local and national. I have learned a lot in that time, which I am trying to pass on, and I have seen linking being done, well and badly, by many. This often leads me to teach about it, and I have been frustrated by the absence of a text and guide for people who are learning about making linkages which covers a useful range of topics.

T_{WO}:
planning and managing linking

MANAGEMENT DECISIONS ABOUT LINKING

Any organisation and any worker in the community, if they are at all active, will find that they are linked with other organisations, informal groups or networks of people in the community. Often, you will decide that you want to have links elsewhere. Many links just grow up in response to a particular need or demand which arises at any one time. However, linking works much better if it is planned. Planning linkages can be for:

- an individual, to help organise their workload more effectively;
- a team, to make sure that they have the appropriate links;
- an organisation, to develop policy about the sort of organisations that its staff should link with;
- any individual relationship, which needs to be well organised.

Management decisions are needed about:

- the aims and priorities of the link;
- methods of linking, which include:
  - the structure of the link
  - the activity involved
  - the role of the linking person
  - linking style
  - linking tactics, and
  - reporting back;
- the timescale of the link;
- the resources available;
- control of linking arrangements.

Many of these points are considered in more detail later in the book. This chapter is simply concerned with thinking about how we can plan a system of links for ourselves, or for our team or organisation.

A useful starting point is to think about where the demand or need to be linked with an organisation comes from. Usually, there are three kinds of demand:

- an existing link which needs to be maintained;
- a request from another organisation for a link;
- a decision you have made that you need a link with another organisation.

The implication of these points is that some links which exist, or are requested may not fit with what you think you need, so perhaps they should not be maintained or set up. On the other hand, a link which you need may not be accepted by the other organisation. This brings us to the first of the management decisions identified above.

AIMS AND PRIORITIES

Why have you got this link, or why do you want it? We often accept links elsewhere, unthinkingly on the assumption that all links are useful, or reject them routinely because they are often more trouble than they are worth. This is about resources: making links uses resources which might be used elsewhere. Some people think that linkages take you away from your main work, others are so keen on co-operation that they always spend the time and money on links.

We can clarify this decision by looking at the aims that may be fulfilled by making links. These can be divided into three groups:

- *Service aims* are concerned with providing services to the public effectively. Good practical relationships with agencies that refer potential clients, accept referrals from you or help clients are essential aspects of linking which meet your service's aims.
- *Maintenance aims* are concerned with keeping the agency in being so that it can meet its service aims. Examples might be regular contact with potential funding agencies such as trusts, or with organisations which have political influence over the environment in which you operate, such as the local authority; if you are in a local authority, you might need the support of other departments, of councillors and of central government departments.
- *Policy aims* are concerned with changing policies in other organisations or in government which affect the clients in the community that you serve.

Policy and maintenance aims are in a way less important than service aims, since they do not bring such immediate dividends, and ethically, we cannot abandon immediate needs in favour of long-term objectives. If policy and maintenance aims are not pursued, there may be no immediate disaster. In the long run, though, our work may be much more difficult and clients' and communities' lives may be much more difficult. So, if the local planning department is ignorant of or hostile to a residents' group in a conservation area, there may be no immediate problems, but if in the future they group wants to stop a large development in their area, the planning department's knowledge of and sympathy with their aims could be very useful.

A useful approach, therefore, is to look at each of the organisation's aims and identify what links might benefit each one. Often, one link will benefit several aims, but these can be divided up into service, maintenance or policy aims and put in order of importance. Table 1 gives an example from a local Age Concern group.

Table 1
Linkage aims in a local Age Concern group

Service	Maintenance	Policy
Local health centre	Social services	Local council
Local social services office	department liaison	for voluntary
Reason:	officer for voluntary	service
professional advice;	organisations	Local MP
referrals;	Secretary, XYZ Trust	National Age
help for clients	*Reason:*	Concern
	funding	*Reason:*
Local social security office		influence on
Reason:	Local councillor	health and
help for clients	*Reason:*	social services
	political support	policy

METHODS

The method of making links affects how you view your aims and priorities and vice versa. Some links involve forming a good relationship which you can then call on as needed or which maintains itself through social contacts or regular work contacts.

If this is easy with one particular organisation or person, the very ease may encourage you to spend time and resources on such links when it should not be so high a priority. Doing the easy things may not bring strong enough dividends in a crisis, and concentrating on the arduous may help you more.

Planning your methods helps to ensure that your priorities are not skewed by such factors. It is also important for building links without a waste of resources. In the following paragraphs, some of the important points are mentioned, but since methods of linking are the subject of the whole of this book most of these points are expanded on in later chapters rather than being dealt with here.

The *structure* of links is about the pattern of contacts which make the link work. The pattern is made up of the number and position of people to be kept in contact, the frequency of contacts and the situation in which they are carried out (e.g. regular formal meetings, social contacts, special approaches at particular times, issuing publications).

The *activities* involved might be attendance at a meeting perhaps only once or perhaps more regularly. It might also involve membership of a committee, public speaking, presenting arguments to a committee, writing letters, press releases, reports and so on.

The *role* of linking persons needs to be considered. How far should they be independent and free to manoeuvre, or constrained by general policies or specific instructions? How far should they be the public incarnation of the organisation (e.g. as the Director of Social services tends to be) and how far its servant (e.g. as the committee administrator tends to be)?

Linking *style* is an important consideration, since approaching the other organisation in ways which are uncomfortable for the linking person or for the target organisation may disrupt relationships or prevent them from developing.

Tactics should be planned, so that you can decide what is the best way to influence an organisation. Perhaps it is simply to keep an eye on things, to have a general influence on its work or to affect a particular decision or activity.

Reporting back will also need to be organised, possibly to a group if you are linking on behalf of a team or organisation, or by keeping records related to your aims if you are linking for your own purposes. Often, linking persons act on behalf of others, who have an interest in what is going on. Keeping effective records and reports which show what you are achieving can often be the only way of testing what results you have achieved.

Table 2 shows the methods identified by a social services area team for their links with the local social security office, which were an issue for them at the time.

TIMESCALE

An important aspect of any human activity, no less of linking work, is the timing of it. *Duration of contacts*, that is how long they continue, may be planned. *Timing markers,* times which may be crucial or target dates that you wish to set, may also be relevant. *Order,* the arrangement in time of events or activities, e.g. which comes before another, is sometimes a consideration. Each of these may be forecast or planned for, and may be relevant to the choice of linking person. For example, if you expect a link to go on for some years, it is unwise to choose a linking person who may not be available for a long period or who gets bored by continuing relationships.

Different timescales may have to be fitted together For example, a general practitioner often expects to deal with patients within a few hours, whereas typically the social services area team may take several days or weeks to deal with a referral. Attempts to build links between the two services will be affected by the differences between them. A specific agreement about timescale may be needed, or the allocation of a worker to respond immediately to the doctor's referrals may be needed so that the timescales can be aligned.

Sometimes, good relationships with one agency may depend on the support of another. A private residential care home, for example, might take the decision to build up relationships with nursing staff in the hospitals in the area where many patients might come from, hoping that a good reputation would make it easier to build links with community nursing staff, which in turn would assist in building a reputation with social services staff. Different strategies, with consequent changes in the ordering of contacts might equally well be imagined.

Timing can also be a pressure on linking persons. Things may have to be hurried as a marker approaches. For instance, if a respite carer has agreed to receive an elderly lady into her home while caring relatives go on holiday, the date of the holiday applies pressure to the arrangements which have to be completed. A programme of getting to know the new home and for carer and elderly lady to get to know each other will have to be planned in

Table 2
Methods of linking used by a social services area team with its local social security office

Structure	Activities	Role	Style	Tactics	Reporting back
TEAM LEADER: quarterly meeting with DSS manager	regular formal meeting contact	nominee	formal	general influence	team meetings after items for discussion recorded in issues book, collected from team meeting prior to contact
DEBT SPECIALIST: frequent contacts with special cases officer at DSS	frequent telephone contacts, occasional formal meetings about particular cases	representative; client advocate	informal, respectful, tenacious	direct influence on specific cases; accumulation of evidence of problems	problems recorded in issues book; periodic discussion at team meetings
SOCIAL WORKERS: frequent contacts by phone on behalf of clients	frequent routine telephone contacts; occasionally accompany clients to DSS office	representative, client advocate	as with debt specialists	as with debt specialists	as with debt specialists

good time. While such pressures may make things more difficult, they can also give structure, purpose and a sense of limitation to a process which otherwise might seem interminable. Thus, without the holiday coming along, a getting-to-know-you process might always be felt to be inadequate, but knowing that for a brief period the move to the respite carer's home will be necessary but that this will not be forever allows the participants in the arrangement to feel comfortable with it. This would be far more difficult if the caring arrangement were for a less specific purpose.

Setting time limits, markers or ordering the linking process can be a good way of helping us keep to objectives, decide on tactics and, in particular, providing the motivation to keep going when nothing seems to work or when relationships become difficult. The corollary of this is the necessity of adhering carefully to set limits.

RESOURCES

Among the most important resources in linking are the skills and interests of the linking persons. A variety of people may be available to do the linking jobs and it is essential to try to fit each linking person to the right job, using their particular skill, experience or status. Sometimes this is made difficult by the appointment process for the linking person, e.g. if a representative is elected, or a specific link is the preserve of a particular office in your organisation. It is worth trying to establish effective forms of appointment which are relevant to the linking tasks in each case. Sometimes election is better if representativeness is needed (in which case, you should pay attention to the right constituency for the election; do not involve people who are not to be represented and aim to involve everyone who will be represented); often selection is better.

Other resources which are relevant are information to back up the work of the linking person, including information about the policy or concerns of your organisation. Expenses may need to be paid (including membership fees, admission fees, perhaps the cost of entertaining or of child care to release a person with young children). Equipment may be needed (e.g. for writing, reporting back) or facilities offered to the other organisation as a result of working together. Thus, an official agency will sometimes offer typing or meeting facilities to an informal group as a mark of their commitment to a relationship, even though this is not strictly necessary. Such moves are often resisted by administrators on grounds of fairness or setting a precedent, and it helps to have a very clear idea of the purpose for offering such resources, which the analysis of your linking activities proposed in this chapter will help you to achieve.

CONCLUSION

This chapter has emphasised the importance of identifying demand and need for linking and planning an organised approach to meeting such demands. An essential part of the management task is to make sure that linking is established through careful planning to achieve the most effective results.

EXERCISES FOR CHAPTER 2

1 Assessing links

A Make a list of the links which you maintain with other organisations, and of requests or needs for links that you can identify. Build this up around
  - a case or situation you are working with or
  - the links you maintain as an individual or
  - the links maintained by your team/organisation.

B In each case identify whether the link
  - exists and
  - was/is the result of a request from the other organisation
  - was/is the result of your decision that you want the link.

C You should now have a list of actual or potential links with a yes/no answer on each of the three points in Section B of the exercise. What does this tell you about your planning of linkages?

D If you are working alone, write down the points that have occurred to you in answering Section C of the exercise. If you are working with others on a personal list, it is useful to share each of your lists and discuss what you can see in each others'. If you are working in a team, having done some sharing, you may find it useful to make explicit some views about team planning for linkages.

2 Assessing the aims of links

A List all the links with other organisations that you have, and should have.

B In each case, decide whether the link meets 'service', 'maintenance' or 'policy' aims, or a combination of these, and the reason why it meets that aim, as in Table 1.

C For each list (service, maintenance, policy) rank the organisations in order of priority for meeting that aim (i.e. top priority = 1; next priority = 2).

D For each organisation, add up the number given under each list to give the priority for linkages for that organisation overall (i.e. the lower the number, the higher the priority).

E If you are working alone, look at each priority ranking, and consider whether it fits with your judgement of the priority. Are there factors which get it a higher or lower priority in the exercise which you are not thinking of in your work? If you are working with others, try sharing your judgements and testing with colleagues the reasons for them. If you are working on a team's links, how do your judgements agree? Are there significant differences in priority? How could you handle this (e.g. by each member taking on links that they personally give high priority to)? Should you be trying to agree priorities?

3 Identifying the methods of linking in use

A Take one (or more) of your priority links, and for each one identify the actual and desired methods for linking (see Table 2 for an example).

B Compare your actual and desired methods, and consider whether you should make any changes in the pattern of your links.

C Does the pattern of your methods show preferences for particular methods of linking? Why is this? Should you change your preferred methods? If you are working in a team, does your team have particular skills, and areas which are underdeveloped?

4 Identifying timescale and resource limitations and requirements

A Take one (or more) of your priority links and for each one identify the timescale of present links, and resources used, and devise a plan of ideal and then likely future timescale and resources.

B Assess and discuss the reasons for variations between past, proposed and ideal timescales and use of resources.

C Consider whether you have enough or appropriate time and resources to do what you want for priority linking activities. Does this assessment affect your priority decisions, or your proposed methods?

Three: liaison

WHAT IS LIAISON?

Liaison is a form of linking in which a representative acts as a 'go-between.' This may be a function which is carried out by committee representatives, but equally often is done outside formal committee arrangements.

It is an arrangement whereby someone is appointed to be the channel of communication and contact between two organisations or individuals. It is usually established where the organisations or individuals recognise that co-operation between them is inadequate in some way. Liaison systems help by giving a focus to co-operation. Sometimes they are reciprocal, so that both sides appoint someone to liaise with the other.

THE LIAISON PROCESS

The first task of a liaison person is information: to gain information about the target organisation, and to give the target organisation information about your own.

Sometimes gaining information may be done by getting published leaflets and guides. Many public, private and voluntary bodies publish annual reports, staff lists, management and committee structures and information about their activities. It may be possible to gain information from lobbying and consumer bodies like the gas and electricity consumer councils, or from independent people with an interest, such as academics in local colleges or universities. The best source of information is likely, however, to be active involvement with the target organisation.

It is useful to find out which individuals in the target organisation should be approached and to establish in their minds that you are the contact for your organisation. As a starting point, it can be helpful to provide them with information about you and your organisation and advise them of times and circumstances in which it is appropriate to contact you. To this end, you could consider, before getting in touch, what information may be useful to them and collect it in readiness, and to plan possible contact arrangements. Decide, for example, when you are most easily available. When it was my job to liaise with a local centre for homeless people on mental health problems, I arranged to be available at my office for three days a week at the time of the doctor's surgery in the morning, and gave my home phone number for any emergencies which arose in the evening as new residents were admitted.

The next stage of liaison work is to establish yourself as *available* in the minds of people in the target organisation or in the person you are liaising with and to get them to have a *positive regard* for you as a contact point. Even if you are not present all the time, you can make it clear when you will be present to deal with enquiries and make yourself psychologically available, by getting people in the target organisation to feel that you are keen to help them and respond to their contacts. In this way, they come to feel good about approaching you, and their anxieties about approaching you and your organisation will recede. This is one of the reasons that I offered my home phone number for the homeless persons centre. It was never needed, but in (somewhat unusually) giving it, I was giving the impression that I would be available in an exceptional way, and this also gave added support to the staff of having someone they knew that they could call on.

One of the difficult points about this early process is responding to inappropriate approaches. The target organisation or person may well respond to you by asking for things that you are not able to offer, and yet you feel it is difficult to refuse because you are trying to build up links. In order to avoid this, it is useful to be clear about the limits of your responsibilities, or to limit the field of liaison, so that you do not have to refuse too many requests, and can do so on the basis of agreed guidelines. The manner of refusal is also important; it is necessary to maintain the view of you as being 'available' and willing to respond positively, even when you have to say 'no.' In linking with a general practice for the first time, one of my staff had a meeting with staff at the centre and discussed the sort of referrals that the doctors might be making. This gave her some idea of what might be coming her way and allowed her to prepare, but also enabled her to say how she would be dealing with things and point out what she could not do. Mixing the positives with the negatives here gave an overall impression of being helpful, while making clear the limits.

As the target organisation or person comes to feel positive about you as a person, this can lead to the problem that they see you as personally helpful, but do not necessarily extend this to the rest of your organisation. Thus, if other people in your organisation have responsibilities which impinge upon the contacts that you are building up, it is helpful to make clear that other people deal with that, and they can be useful too, even though you are the *channel* of contacts.

When passing things on to others, it remains the responsibility of the liaison person to make sure that things go well, particularly in the early stages of contact. The liaison person *progresses* requests from the target organisation through their own organisation and makes sure that they are dealt with adequately, and preferably quickly. This involves either a system whereby all referrals are made to the liaison person and they push them through the system, or a system of reporting to the liaison person from your own agency or from the agency with which there is liaison.

LIAISON SYSTEMS

The next stage of liaison is to set up liaison systems. These can either be to deal with a particular problem or issue, and may therefore be time-limited, or they can be systems which are designed to continue for some time and enhance relationships between the organisations or individuals generally. These two types of system can support one another. Successfully dealing with an issue together cements a long-term relationship. Good long-term relationships make it easier to deal with problems and issues.

One important type of system is a regular arrangement for *passing information*. It is important that the information passed is significant and useful to the other and that they are aware of ways of using it to their benefit, otherwise the exercise may seem sterile. The best information exchanges are about activities which the two organisations or individuals are actively engaged in. If information is received under a liaison arrangement, it helps the relationship develop if you do something with the information received and feed back what happened. The target organisation can then feel, through *feedback*, that they were helpful to you and that you actually responded to them. It may also be useful to identify where information being passed is not fully used, and either make arrangements to use it properly, or discuss with the target organisation whether it would be better to stop the effort of supplying the information, or to organise to supply it in a way that can be used. For example, I once dealt with a liaison system between a social services area team and a housing office about arrears. The initial approach was with a list of people in arrears, but this was later modified to a regular meeting to discuss problem cases which really needed active help, since the practical response to many of the cases on the routine list was virtually nil.

Another aspect of liaison systems is a regular *check* with the target organisation to see if any action is needed. A regular contact prevents crises or difficulties from escalating and emphasises you or your organisation's availability and preparedness to help or be involved.

Sometimes it is useful to have a regular liaison *meeting* to discuss matters of mutual concern. This can help to establish good personal relationships, and put faces to voices at the end of the telephone. It is far more difficult to be obstructive when faced with someone rather than contact by letter or telephone. Liaison meetings should have significant topics to discuss and be held at a sensible frequency so that they are not thin or over-burdened. Otherwise, relationships can be harmed because the meeting becomes an irrelevant talk-shop or never seems to deal with the problems raised. I once took part in a useful regular meeting between social services staff and the local social security office. Initially this was held monthly, but, as we established contacts, fewer issues of principle came up and we agreed to a frequency of every three months, with many practical problems being sorted out by telephone using the personal relationships established.

Joint projects or activities may also be planned and are a good way of accomplishing a particular aim which involves one or more organisations or individuals, but which do not require long-standing liaison systems to be established.

PLANNING LIAISON

Organisations and individuals dealing with a lot of contacts should assess from time to time the range of contacts that they have, and consider whether a liaison system would promote better co-operation.

In Chapter 2, organisations were divided into those where you have service, maintenance and policy aims for being represented therein. In listing groups with which you wish to consider liaison systems, classifying them in this way helps to clarify your aims.

Then, you can identify particular kinds of liaison system which would benefit these aims. For example, the regular exchange of information and identifying key contacts might be appropriate for service aims, since here you may be seeking to refer people between you or respond to particular problems. Maintenance aims might require a regular joint meeting. Policy aims might be better met by a planned joint project with a time limit.

In the same way that representation is planned, by looking at aims, methods, timescale, resources and management control, liaison can be much strengthened by a planned approach.

EXERCISES FOR CHAPTER 3

1 Checking liaison arrangements and aims

A List every organisation with which you have regular liaison arrangements.

B For each organisation list the aims which you have in maintaining the arrangements.

C Classify your aims into 'service', 'maintenance' and 'policy' aims.

D Evaluate whether your aims for each organisation are appropriate.

2 Liaison processes

A For each organisation with which you have liaison arrangements, identify the liaison person(s).

B For each person, identify the stage reached in the development of liaison processes:
- information
- first approach
- availability and positive regard
- channels established
- progressing issues
- liaison systems established.

C In each case, evaluate whether what has been achieved is appropriate.

3 Liaison systems

A For each organisation for which a liaison system exists, identify the sort of system in use:
- information passing
- feedback
- regular check
- regular meeting (and its frequency)
- joint projects.

B In each case, evaluate whether what has been achieved is appropriate.

F our:
first approaches

FIRST APPROACHES ARE IMPORTANT

In any linking activity, you are going to have to deal with making a first approach to another organisation, and that means an approach to another person. The first approach often has an unreasonably strong influence on what happens subsequently - a mess made at the start can be hard to recover from. So, first approaches are often worth planning with some care. This second chapter in the group dealing with various liaison skills therefore concentrates on this aspect of linking.

The aim of the first approach is to persuade the other that it is worth going on with the relationship, and that it will benefit both of you.

THE RIGHT PERSON

First, make contact with the right person. In many cases, if you arrive at the wrong point in an organisation, you will be passed on to the right place. But you cannot guarantee this; the person you deal with may be too busy or not know enough about you or your problem or their own organisation to get it right. You also run the risk of irritating them or looking inept (and therefore possibly less trustworthy for the future) if you get it wrong. It also boosts your confidence in dealing with a strange organisation to feel you are making the correct approach.

Finding the right contact can be achieved by asking outsiders who are likely to know, by doing research into an organisation from leaflets or other published material, by making covert enquiries to the organisation or by making a preliminary approach.

Relevant outsiders might be other members of the organisation that you know, or other organisations that are already in contact with your target, or organisations which specialise in knowing who to contact, for example the local council for voluntary service (whose job is to help voluntary groups, so they often know about voluntary and community groups and the right people to approach in relevant state organisations, the local library or information services, or the citizens advice bureau. Many organisations (especially government agencies) have formal structures and publish advice on whom to contact.

The advantage of doing this in advance is to get some information about likely reactions to your approach, the best means of approach, and the attitudes and perhaps personal foibles of those whom you will contact. Do not take others' views too seriously, however, since for one thing their judgement may not be very acute. Also, their organisation may carry a different, and more or less favourable, connotation for the target organisation.

Beware of old-fashioned local government departments which only list the name of the chief officer, and all letters are signed as though they come from him (it usually is a 'him'). Such departments get a surprising number of calls asking to speak to this person, which have to be sorted out by telephonists and secretaries. You can sometimes avoid this by looking at the top or bottom of the note which says 'if telephoning, ask for...' or 'officer dealing with this matter...'.

If this fails look for a typing reference (or nowadays a word processing file reference). You will often see something (occasionally part of a longer reference that includes a file number) that looks like this: 'ABC/DEF' or 'ABC/def' or 'ABC...' followed by a number. Usually these first initials are of the person dealing with the matter, and the second group are those of the typist. You can telephone, say you have a letter with this reference and ask to talk to whoever that is.

Alternatively, you can make enquiries first. Telephone the office, explain what you are calling about, and ask to speak to the right person or department. It is quite acceptable to ask for the name and title of the person you are put through to; or to ask them directly. Some organisations nowadays require their staff to wear name labels. Equally, there are some government departments that refuse to give names, on the shameful grounds that this is asking for their staff to be victimised. Presumably this reflects the knowledge that they have a form of organisation or policies which, when their staff implement them, lead to victimisation.

If you prefer to approach someone you know or whose name

you have been given, you can hedge your bets by asking for the name you have been given, explaining briefly what it is about and checking that they are the right person before going on. Most agencies are happy with this approach.

If you need to find out the right person covertly, either because telephoning and asking is resisted or because you have forgotten or lost a brief previous contact, ask a woman to telephone and say they are 'Mr Green's secretary' and they have to address a letter, who should they address it to? They will usually get the full name, job title, address and any honorifics. This sort of thing goes on all the time between secretaries rescuing their bosses.

THE RIGHT IMAGE

The second matter to consider is the image you wish to present on first contact.

On the telephone this is a matter of voice and to some extent job title. The essential thing is for this to be appropriate. In Britain, being class-ridden, it is sometimes hard for someone with a rough or heavy regional accent to get put through to important people. Middle class southern accents with conventional pronunciation get through the barriers more easily. Sometimes emphasising your job title ('I am chairman of the Southgate Community Association') or the nature or importance of the matter will help. Calmness and reasonableness might get you a hearing, whereas evident anger and aggression may well be sidetracked on the telephone (unless you have the manner and accent to command attention).

In many cases, these are not things to worry about. A light regional accent is not usually a bar, particularly in its locality. In the case of a community group, anything other than a local accent might imply that it is run by professionals or some middle class clique and is not truly representative.

Similarly, when meeting people, it is important that class and presentation are appropriate. You should avoid trying to over-impress or to be something you are not, although having made a special effort sometimes causes people to feel you have taken trouble over meeting them, so they will take trouble over you.

For the same reason, ruffled hair, unkempt appearance or uncleanliness never impress favourably, whether you usually wear jeans or suits. There are some circles in which it is unacceptable to wear jeans, just as there are some where you would be considered as 'weird' if you wore a suit. You will be expected to wear what is appropriate to your circle, and to dress up a bit if you are making a very formal representation to senior and important people.

It may seem objectionable to make these points. I am afraid, though, I have sat with people in all sorts of different circles after hearing representations and found that the message even of trained and qualified professional staff in some representative capacity has, in private, after the meeting, often been obscured by comments about how scruffy or ill-mannered the representative was. Equally, at the other end of the scale, I have seen quite reasonable presentations rejected with comments about 'poncy middle-class jerks in suits'.

I dress up or down for meetings, but not so far as to discredit either my middle class accent or my community role. Although I'm afraid I seem naturally to cause the cut and form of clothes to become shapeless, I try to be tidy at least at the start of meetings.

Another important aspect of image is being able to offer the conventional courtesies, and giving an impression of openness or preparedness to act on what is done in the contact. A remote attitude, refusal to go to the pub afterwards accept or offer coffee, or a need to refer everything back and refusals to take anything at face value often obstruct future contacts.

On the other hand I have seen a very experienced lobbyist convey very clearly to a minister the anger of the people he was representing simply by stubbornly calling him 'Secretary of State' after every few sentences, while the Secretary of State was assiduously calling everyone by the forenames that were conventional in the setting. And everything retained the appropriate veneer of total courtesy.

Many representative situations have this element of games-playing about them. Ordinary linking may not be quite the same; less stylised behaviour is appropriate. Nonetheless, the importance and effect of image emphasises the importance of playing properly whatever drama you are performing for the benefit of the people on whose behalf you are linking.

One element which is not games-playing and is increasingly important to many people is presenting an attitude which does not 'put down' the people you are dealing with. Some readers, for instance, will have been brought up short by the example, given above of the 'chairMAN' of the Community Association, others will have taken it for granted. This is called 'gender-specific language' because it identifies the title of a (relatively powerful) role with one (the male) sex. In many situations, it will be expected that you are careful about how you use words that identify ethnic origins or disability. But the words are only the surface issue, because they represent in you an underlying attitude towards equality between the sexes, races and between disabled and non-disabled people. In some social services circles, you will be regarded as offensive if your language is sexist, racist or 'disablist'. In some more conventional circles, you will be regarded as a joke if you go out of your way to use non-gender-specific or non-ethnocentric (not centred on any particular ethnic group) language. You will have to make a decision about how far you can be tactical about a usage which may be second nature to you, indeed may be an important matter of principle.

This draws attention to an important issue in linking work, generally, about how far it is appropriate or right to present yourself in a way which is not really you in order to achieve some objective with people whom you would not usually come across. My own view is that you should never compromise your principles. So, using this issue as an example, I would carry on using 'chair' and 'chairperson' rather than 'chairman' and defend it even if someone were making fun of me. But I think it is also right to be courteous, so I would not ram the point down somebody's throat if they really find it offensive. Similarly, I would never go to the point of dishonesty in presentation, even though I would do my best to meet the needs of the other person. I think this is essential to helping meet the needs of the person or organisation I am representing. They might not be able to afford my principles. On the other hand, they might not be willing to accept my compromise of their principles. You must use your judgement, but the important thing is to be aware of the issue and do something about it.

THE RIGHT SUBJECT

The third important aspect of making the first approach is coming up with the right subject for a starting point. It must be sufficiently interesting and worthwhile for the other person to bother about. On the other hand, it should not be so potentially difficult that they will be put off.

Ideally, you should have a joint interest which will benefit you both (e.g. applying for a grant together, stopping someone doing something you both dislike, dealing with a problem that you both have). Alternatively, you should have something tangible that you can offer them (e.g, information contacts, resources, money, reduced hassle). In particular, reducing conflict or difficulty that you have been experiencing in your relationship is a tangible benefit. You can say 'Look, things have been difficult between us; why don't we get together and sort something out?'

Sometimes there are substantial problems in your past relationship which are likely to be off-putting. If you are aware of them, no doubt the other party will be, so it is best to acknowledge these, while offering a real commitment to dealing with them, and perhaps show a clear starting point where you have some shared interests.

THE RIGHT RESOURCES

Finally, part of presenting a good first impression is having the right resources - the information and materials that you can provide. An important example is considering in advance what information will be necessary for an effective interaction and how it can best be presented. You need to prepare in advance for any likely questions. You might have a folder of leaflets ready. You need to be prepared to answer problems that are raised with you.

If you are meeting to propose some joint venture or activity, you need to work out what you or your agency can offer, and ideally get authority to make the offers. So, in approaching an agency for help with a particular client, be clear as to what you are going to do, and specifically how you would like the agency to fit in with this to make their contribution. Also, you need to have information ready to demonstrate your own contribution. This will help to overcome anxieties in the other agency that your proposal will involve them in doing more than your plan expects.

EXERCISES FOR CHAPTER 4

1   Assessing an organisation for the right approach

A   Identify one or more organisations to which you want to make an approach; and, as a check, identify one or more organisations where you already have links.

B   For each organisation you don't know, identify the right person(s), image(s), issue(s) and resource(s) to make a first approach to that organisation.

C   For each organisation that you do know, identify an issue that you want to take up with them, and again identify the right person, image, issue and resources within that organisation to make the approach. See if you can draw a diagram of the connections between your present contacts and the approach you are going to make.

D   Role play the first approach - if you can, find out a bit about the person being approached, so that their player can be as realistic as possible.

E   Following each first approach, review its success.

2   Reviewing the approachability of you or your own organisation

A   Identify a number of organisations that might approach you (if you are acting as an individual) or your organisation. Identify the person(s), image(s), issue(s) and resource(s) that they might present and what your response would be.

B   Role play a number of possible approaches.

C   If you are a team or organisation, review a list of organisations that might approach you and likely topics of approach, and work out the persons within your organisation and team that they should be directed to.

3   Looking at yourself

A   Examine the image you (as an individual - if you are working on this as a team, everyone should do this privately) present to others when you approach them, and that they receive when they approach you. To give this some focus, you may want to assess how you did in one particular recent situation.

B   In both cases, list any improvements you want to make. If you are working as a team, you may want to share this in pairs, and then the pairs can share their findings with the whole team.

C   Role play a recent situation, trying out the improvements you have made in your approach, and see what the difference is.

4   Difficult situations

A   Think of the most difficult situation you are likely to face.

B   Analyse why it is difficult; this may include things about you, about the other person or organisation, or the subject that you think you might have to approach them with.

C   Think of three ways that you could improve how you could deal with each of the difficulties.

D   How about trying it out?

Five:
linking styles

PERSONAL STYLE AND APPROACH

Linking work is strongly affected by the style with which it is carried out. Not every matter can be resolved by strategy and planning; what also counts is how links are developed and promoted.

Some aspects of style are associated with the personality and approach of the person doing the linking. Since linking is done by a person, the influence of their personality and character sometimes comes to be associated with the task. If their way of doing things is seen as having some consistency over a period, it comes to be associated with them as a personal style. Sometimes this is seen as more important to success than resources or structures, because of the personal nature of the linking task. Thus, successful links are felt to come about because of the comfortable personality or flexible approach of the representative. However, to some extent, all tasks in human and organisational relationships reflect both the personal style of the participants and many other features of the situation, which are considered in later parts of this chapter.

Another important feature of the person or the representative is their *approach*. This is the way in which they typically consider issues and how they initiate discussion or action about problems. For example, some people approach a problem by thinking out all its complexities before acting, others like to get involved in action, and take up each issue as it arises. Obviously a mixture of these and other approaches are common.

PATTERNS AND STRUCTURES

How linking takes place is also affected by existing patterns and structures of communication and linking. Where a history exists, the linking which is done must respond to what has happened in the past. Where this is complex, it should be disentangled and studied. It can be helpful for a new representative to start out by simplifying a structure which has grown up over a period.

Patterns are consistent ways in which approaches have been made elsewhere, and typical responses which have resulted. Often effective linking becomes inhibited by conventional responses between organisations or individuals. Rather than being relevant to the present situation, they can lead to assumptions and prejudices getting in the way of appropriate action on the present issue.

For example, there was an arrangement between one social services area team and the local housing department whereby information about tenants causing problems for the housing department were referred to the area team. Over a period, this had settled down to a system of information about tenants in rent arrears, which were checked in the area team, whose staff responded to problems with those clients who were part of their existing caseload. In the housing department, this response was seen as limited and self-interested, and was not effective in helping them with other tenants who actually presented the housing department with personal difficulties. When the area team decided to appoint a liaison social worker to deal with perceived problems on a large council estate, the past history got in the way of building up positive relationships, since housing staff did not see that the liaison worker would be interested in helping to resolve their difficulties, and the liaison worker started off from an assumption that housing staff were not interested in anything but rent arrears.

Structures are about formal systems for liaison and communication. These can also obstruct or facilitate the development of links. For example, a system that all problems with a particular agency should be raised through a formal committee can prevent informal resolution of problems, which may then fester and be hard to resolve in the formal surroundings of the committee room. Equally, the presence of close friendly relationships between agencies' staff can prevent the formal resolution of issues which require confrontation and conflict. As a result, clients' rights to a service may become compromised because the professionals involved do not want to upset existing relationships.

Very often, personal relationships in linking require a balance of formality and informality, and of pleasantness and confrontation, and the existence of any regular pattern or structure can inhibit flexibility in linking. On the other hand, a relatively open pattern and structure can facilitate contacts which will resolve problems.

Achieving openness of pattern and structure requires explicit planning of these features of representation. When establishing any system of communication, therefore, it can be useful to set up regular reviews of how they are developing and each side's response to the way in which contacts have developed, as well as the content of the problems that have arisen. It is important to stick to the plan of making regular reviews. Otherwise, there is a tendency to feel that everything is going well without realising that other parties to the links are not having their needs met.

This is particularly crucial in developing packages of care in a community setting, because clients and carers may feel inhibited from raising problems when they see that the worker has gone to a lot of trouble to set the links up. They may also not have a clear perception of what is wrong, and have, rather, a faint feeling of unease, which eventually grows to dissatisfaction. In building such links, therefore, setting up patterns and structures for communication is a crucial step, as is reviewing regularly how they are working. For example, where three neighbours are co-operating in the care of an elderly lady, it might be agreed that they sit down and create a weekly diary. The worker would then need to review how this process was working for the participants, in case for example, one felt dominated by others into not being able to present their views.

SETTING AND MEDIUM

Representative style varies with the setting in which the links take place and the medium of communication. Face-to-face meetings of individuals or small groups usually benefit from a relaxed informal style of conversation. In some cases, though, where authority and power are used to gain influence, a more formal or tense style (or confrontation for instance) may be appropriate. For example, where a worker is meeting with a group of offenders to review offending behaviour, a more formal approach may be required.

Larger meetings, such as committees and case conferences, or formal presentations to groups, often require more organised behaviour, or they may disintegrate into confusion. Here, rather than relying on a shared understanding of what is to be done, procedures such as a formal agenda and speaking through the chair may be appropriate.

Medium also affects linking mechanisms. Speaking on the telephone, for example, while it is often informal, requires particular clarity to describe exactly who you are and to explain at times how you are responding to the points the other person is making. Because they cannot judge by your physical reactions, it is necessary to be clear about whether you are concerned or pleased by what they say.

Effective representation, then, requires careful planning of the setting and medium of representation to enhance what you want to achieve. Formality and informality, prosaic and original, stimulating and laid back: whichever you want to be requires consideration of the best setting and medium for achieving it.

INTRUSION AND INVOLVEMENT

All representation is a balance of *intrusion* and *involvement*. You are setting out from your position to intrude upon the position of another person. In order to achieve this, you have to get involved with the other without losing your loyalty to the person you represent. Yet your involvement, because it is always obviously on behalf of another person or organisation, is always to some extent felt as an intrusion by whoever is receiving your representations. You are trying to get them to change their stance over a particular issue, or to limit their freedom of action and decision-making by accepting your representations about your client's or organisation's needs. If you were not intruding, they would be free to follow their own line.

Representation also requires you to manage your own feelings about intrusion. On the one hand, you may feel diffident about seeking your ends; on the other, you may be angry or emotional about what you are trying to achieve. In the first case, you may not intrude or get involved enough; in the other, you may provoke an adverse reaction by being over-intrusive.

There is also the problem of being and becoming involved with another organisation or person, as you begin to negotiate on behalf of your client or your organisation. Inevitably, you begin to take on some responsibility for the effects of what you are asking of the other organisation or individual, but you must also stand back from this if you are to represent appropriately.

My general approach to these issues is that a representative should concentrate on being clear about their own role and position, and should try to achieve a shared clarity with others about the pattern, structure and style of links which exist or that they wish to achieve. It is also necessary to be well-informed about the organisations or individuals and their situations which you are trying to link, so careful study and preparation is essential to good linking. You must always be open to some active involvement in the other organisation or with the individual and their needs because, in a negotiation, only by meeting their needs will you find ways of moving forward.

What should be avoided is diffidence, which can feel to others as though you have nothing to offer by way of involvement, or a take-it-or-leave-it approach, which can seem aggressively intrusive, or aggressively uninvolving.

CONFLICT AND CONFRONTATION

There is a distinction between aggression, conflict and confrontation. Very often, a disagreement can be resolved or defused by a shared exploration of the problem, as we shall see in Chapter 7. Confrontation and conflict need not be aggressive. Confrontation is the explicit presentation to another of the areas of disagreement between you, and can be done with courtesy and firmness. Conflict derives from actions taken to enforce your view in the situation - you are actually acting against one another. This can be helpful, by forcing the other to respond to the issues that you are presenting. On the other hand, it may become destructive as people concentrate on winning conflicts rather than resolving the issue.

Straight talking, therefore, needs to be leavened with an explicit appreciation and acceptance of the problems which are leading to the difficulty, and an active preparedness to become involved in resolving them. Courtesy is always needed alongside openness and persistence. A touch of humour sometimes helps because it humanises you and makes it hard to treat you as an enemy, but you should not allow it to become bitter or sarcastic.

One approach to criticising others is self-deprecation. You say things like 'I'm not sure I understand what is going on...' or 'I'm not sure I'm right...' or 'I'm only new but...' While this makes offering criticisms easier, it can sometimes blunt their force, because some people may feel that it is not important or is not given from a position of strength. Self-deprecation does not work especially when there is a power struggle going on - again persistent and firm comment is needed in such a situation.

Confrontation is dealt with at greater length in Chapter 7 on 'When things go wrong'.

CONCLUSION

This chapter draws attention to the importance of thinking about how a linking person should behave towards others when doing linking work. In particular, a balance will be needed between intrusion and involvement in the other organisation or individual and the issues they face in dealing with your representation. A careful approach is needed to situations in which conflict or confrontation is required or apparent.

EXERCISES FOR CHAPTER 5

1 Assessing personal style

A   Make a list of words which describe your typical style in approaching a situation in which you represent the interests of an organisation or individual to another.

B   For each of your descriptive words about your style, write down a sentence which is typical of something you would say when representing an individual or organisation and which demonstrates how you apply that particular point of style.

2 Evaluating style in practice

A   Write down a brief account of a situation in which you recently represented an individual or organisation.

B   Identify three crucial interventions in the representation, and write down as precisely as you can what you said or did, and how that affected the events.

C   In each case, write down at least one alternative way of dealing with that situation.

D   If possible, share your accounts with another person/your team and discuss what alternative approaches might have been taken.

3 Assessing pattern and structure

A   Select a linkage which is a priority for yourself and your team. Write down every contact which you/your team have had in that linkage over the past year.

B   Identify any typical patterns of contact or response, failures to contact or respond, and any formal structures in place with the link.

C   If possible, investigate with other parties to the link what their perceptions of the arrangements are.

D   If possible, consider with another person/your team what changes in pattern and structure might be desirable, and identify how they might be achieved in co-operation with the other parts of the link.

4 Dealing with conflict/confrontation

A   Identify a situation in which you recently had to confront or get into conflict with someone/another organisation, and write a description of what happened. Divide it into a series of stages which show the progression of the conflict/ confrontation.

B Looking at each stage of the conflict/confrontation, rate in each case on a scale of 1 to 5 (1 - lowest, 5 - highest) the extent to which you were, at that stage of the conflict, intruding and involving yourself in the other organisation or the problems that that individual had in responding to your representations. At each stage, consider whether you could and should have intruded/involved yourself less or more. Write an account of how you could have acted in a better way, if possible sharing this with another person/your team for their views.

C Role play the conflict/confrontation based on your improved approach.

Six:
preparation and training for linking work

THE NEED FOR PREPARATION AND TRAINING

Too often, we throw ourselves into liaison, representation and co-ordination activities as a sideline from our main work of helping clients or caring for our relative or friend. But linking is not a sideline, it is a crucial part of helping and needs careful preparation. As part of their planning, organisations need to prepare and train their staff and volunteers in making the connections that will achieve their policy objectives. In planning services for an individual, too, the people involved cannot just set a programme of care. They need to make sure that everyone who is involved understand and is ready to play his/her part. The problems are very similar, so in this chapter I look at each form of preparation in relation to representation between organisations, and then between people who are working together to care for an individual person.

PREPARATION

The first requirement is *information*. In building links between organisations, linkers need to have sufficient information about their own organisation and its policies to present it properly, and they need to know enough about the target organisation to make the best approach.

Policy information and factual material about your own organisation will help a representative to make points which support your policy and enhance your representative's status by being correct. You cannot assume that even an experienced member of your staff, still less a volunteer or committee member, is fully aware of policy and activities throughout the organisation. They often only know about their own part of it, or have a particular viewpoint which may not be helpful to the target organisation. Documents, such as reports, previous minutes, correspondence or policy statements will all help. Sometimes a briefing or opportunity for debate from someone who is knowledgeable about the topic, or from the team whose view is being represented can be helpful.

I once met an active committee member for an organisation for people with handicaps of which I was a member. He had been to a meeting of similar organisations to discuss the local authority's grant aid arrangements, and felt that he had not done very well. At the meeting, among other things, he had been asked whether our organisation also helped people with sensory handicaps (associated with sight and hearing) for which there were other specialised organisations which were not so well grant-aided. He had not known what the agreed borderlines were, having never come across the problem, since his interest in our organisation had arisen from having a physically handicapped wife. In this case, having clear, full information about the organisation was crucial to representing its interests properly, making the representative comfortable with his role, and being fair to the other relevant organisations. Both he and the organisation had assumed that his experience was sufficient, without careful thought in advance of what byways of concern might arise at the meeting.

Information about the target organisation can be offered in similar ways. The representative needs to know about the current issues and work of the organisation, so that she/he can get started quickly and make an impact. Having such information also gives the representative confidence in you and in his/her work. Clarity about the purpose of the representation, ways of making a start and who to contact may be useful. Making arrangements for support, especially in the early stages, and reporting back can give a new representative confidence.

In one social services area team, for example, a worker was given the role of liaison with a local general practice of three doctors, one of whom was known to be hostile to social workers. The liaison worker was most anxious about the early contacts, especially when it appeared that the irascible doctor had little time for her. The team, therefore, collected information about their main active cases with the practice, sought help from the health visitor attached to the practice, who was well-known to them, and also collected systematic information about recent contacts with all the doctors.

Clear information is also required in linking up the people involved in caring for an individual person. Everyone who is helping needs to know who else is taking part and how to contact them. They need to know what everybody's job is, and why, and how they fit together. Again, written information can be useful, perhaps in the form of a timetable, a 'contract' or a handing over diary, so that everyone has a record of what happened in the time before they got involved.

The second need in preparation is to make *contacts and relationships*. Again, both your own and the target organisation should be reviewed for contacts which will be useful for the representative. In your own organisation anyone who can connect the representative to information or guidance about policy or the host organisation and anyone who can facilitate feedback into your organisation may be useful. The target organisation may only have one starting point for contacts, such as a liaison officer, secretary, treasurer or director. Equally, there may be people who can ease the transition into the organisation. In the long term, useful points of influence or sources of information can be identified in advance for the benefit of your representative, and contact and introductions made on their behalf. This was the reason for the work with the health visitor in the example given above.

People working to help individual clients similarly need their contacts and relationships properly established. They need to know who to contact and the right approach to take when there are problems. If possible, you could make an early introduction so that they can feel confident in approaching someone. Sometimes potential contacts can be forewarned that they might receive an approach. One useful bit of help is to give clients in this situation a little booklet listing likely contacts. Better still, work with them on creating their own list, and make the explorations of the network of contacts together, because this involves them more.

All these preparations help to meet a third need, often forgotten, *confidence-building*. It can be a very lonely and isolating responsibility to represent one organisation to another, and to take the burden of caring for someone who may be in danger if things go wrong. People can very easily feel cut off from friendliness and contacts.

Being a representative in another organisation is, in a sense, to enter a new world, leaving behind a familiar one. New loyalties may be required. If the process has been planned there may be objectives to be met; you hope not to let down the people who have trusted you as their representative. People in your organisation can help by offering a regular review of how things are going, and a chance to talk over any problems and to see that their work is valued.

Dealing with helpers in individual cases presents very similar problems. There is the feeling of responsibility, lack of support, risk of letting you and the other carers or the client down. Again, you can offer regular review, a chance to talk over any feelings, reassurance that insecurity about responsibility is often shared by everyone in the situation. It may assist helpers if you carry out with them a realistic appraisal of the skills and experience they are bringing to the task which you and the person being cared for value. People often unreasonably underrate what they offer.

TRAINING

Part of the preparation may lead you to recognise that the representative or carer does not have the necessary skills and experience. In this case, various kinds of training may help. One sort of training offers *knowledge* that the representative or carer may not have. Other training can offer development in *skills* which may be helpful in their work. Third, training may sometimes offer help in confidence-building, attitude or values which will strengthen a person's capacity to do the job.

For example, if a representative is making contact with an organisation for mentally ill people, or with an individual who is mentally ill, they may need to become aware of their own attitudes towards and fears of mental illness. Some people unconsciously stigmatise or patronise others, or can find relationships with mentally ill people difficult because they have fears about what they will be like. Awareness and acceptance of their present feelings and ways in which they can change and gain fuller understanding may be needed. People need to convey the right attitude in themselves before they can convince others that they are genuine.

The types of training that may be possible include:

- information packs with a series of exercises that people can work through, alone or with a group;
- internal training courses run by your own staff;
- specially created external training (e.g. at local colleges);
- standard courses offered by educational institutions and agencies such as the Open University;
- courses run by training departments of local agencies;
- a course of reading and study;
- a small, internal discussion group.

Various kinds of skills training may also be useful. For representatives between organisations skills in the following may be relevant:

- meetings procedures;
- presenting arguments, negotiating;
- group work, recognising conflicts, group feeling;
- assertiveness training.

For people working in caring, training can be offered in specific skills relevant to the job such as:

- lifting, physical care, minor nursing;
- planning and co-operation;
- knowing about approaching services which are helpful.

EXAMPLES OF PREPARATION

A particularly helpful form of preparation and training is to arrange a period of induction into the host organisation and introduction to people and issues within it. A programme of visits, conversations with important people and opportunities to observe relevant activities are all helpful.

Training can usefully take in aspects of the host organisation or your own which provide a background to the representative role. One organisation I worked with provided representatives on a local authority committee, for example. They arranged for new representatives to attend a complete cycle of sub-committees leading to the main committee and council meeting. One topic of interest was followed through the whole cycle, to see how it was dealt with. In between, there were talks to the local authority officer concerned with the issue, to see what work she was involved with in between. In this way, they could follow a decision from its inception through all the stages.

The following example is about training informal carers in an individual situation. A woman suffering from various disabilities caused by multiple sclerosis was mainly cared for by her husband, who was becoming ill with the stress. Two other rather distant relatives agreed to help, and the community nursing service arranged some informal instruction on basic nursing tasks, which the husband had learned by example as his wife's condition had worsened. The social services also explained the network of services that they could call on and gave them a list of contacts, putting all three helpers in touch with a local support group.

HANDING OVER

Many new linking people, as in the last example, are replacing old ones, and it is important to organise the handover properly. It is easy to assume that things will just pick up as they were going along, and to forget the great deal of knowledge and expertise which was built up by predecessors.

There are many feelings involved. For the leaving linker, there may be relief, or regret, or feelings of loss, or rejection (especially if they have lost an election). They may need further opportunities for involvement. We have looked at feelings of fear and trepidation for people who are starting out. However, some starters may be doing it as a duty or a bore and will need galvanising and motivation.

Leaving or resigning representatives should be encouraged to provide some briefing notes about what was going on in another organisation. Similarly, people taking a role with an individual need to be explicit about their timetable and actions - they will have fallen into a pattern which the person that they are helping will have become accustomed to. Style and strategy, particular tips about little things that help, or people to beware of all help a successor.

Ideally, notes should be supplemented by a meeting, or joint involvement for a while. With organisations, old and new linkers can attend together (special dispensations from constitutions) may be needed for this; with individual caring, they can act together for a while. In doing this, however, it is important to avoid new relationships being damaged by old conflicts. A new linker needs to make their own decisions, informed by the aims of the linking activity and any guidance from your organisation or other people involved in individual caring.

EXERCISES FOR CHAPTER SIX

1 Working on a training programme for linkers on behalf of an organisation

A Create a list of all linking people with other organisations.

B Ideally, involve existing linkers in identifying needs for knowledge about the target organisation, important people to link with, strategies and tactics, skills needed and emotions, philosophy and attitude that are relevant. If this is not possible, try to make your own list.

C Identify ways of preparing people for meeting each of these identified needs. Again, involve others if you can. Then create a programme, preferably containing practical activities - people like to learn by doing, and they like to get on with their task, not to sit around learning.

D Consider what points of learning need reinforcement, and when that will be needed. Will the effectiveness of learning need to be monitored (e.g. by seeing how effective welfare rights representation has been with a social security office that has been targeted) and training repeated or changed?

E Consider what implications the experience of providing the training, and the reactions of the people involved will have for you and other people involved in the management of an organisation, and how you will arrange to have these taken up.

2 Working on a training programme for linkers in an individual case

A Undertake Exercise 1, substituting a group of linkers in an individual case.

3 Planning a handover strategy

A List existing linking activities (either with organisations or in an individual case), and create a list of each person involved.

B For each individual, write down who would be a suitable substitute in
i. a temporary emergency
ii. a permanent replacement.

C In each case, make a list of knowledge, skills and attitudes that are likely to be or are actually required (if possible involve those who already have the linking role) and work out a programme for handover.

Seven:
when things go wrong

Linkages always involve personal relationships, and inevitably things sometimes go wrong and a useful relationship is upset. This chapter is about preventing and recovering from problems.

PREVENTION

In most organisations, groupings of people concerned with shared interests and in particular services, gossip is rife. It is hard to keep things secret (and often there is no good reason to do so) and it is impossible to stop people speculating about others' motivations and interests. Often, events, mistakes, statements and all their possible implications are passed around, embroidered, expanded, misunderstood and twisted out of recognition. Payne's law on this subject says:

Payne's Law
If any activity will be disadvantaged or any person discomforted by the revelation of confidential information, then it will be conveyed to the person most likely to respond adversely by communications which are most likely to cast the most destructive information in a form most likely to be misunderstood in the most disastrous way.

Sensible people involved in linking take precautions against these likelihoods. One obvious preventative is to express what you want to say as clearly as possible. Where it is likely to be controversial, ask listeners to repeat it back so that you can be sure that they have interpreted it correctly. Say something like 'I wonder if I've got this point across properly - how do you see it?' Confirming what you say in letters and minutes is also useful.

Less obviously, it is a valuable skill to control what you say, by considering how it might be misinterpreted (because if it might be, it probably will be). You can then put it in a different way, or several ways to emphasise your perception of the point. If it is controversial, can you avoid saying it at all? Where total avoidance is not possible, act on the assumption that the information will almost certainly get back to people who should not receive it and plan ways of heading off the resultant problems or prepare your defences for when you are faced with the matter. Again, a written record or notes of what you actually did say can lend your denials some credibility. And if you get no adverse response, you can bask in a warm feeling of relief.

Another preventative is to choose your audiences and confidants carefully so that they do not include people whose interests are inimical to yours or at least they have some integrity. From others' points of view, it is worth cultivating the practice of not passing on information which might be disadvantageous to someone, or make it clear when you are given information that you have different interests and your concerns are not in tune with theirs. If you are obliged to pass on damaging information, at least you can help people who might suffer from this act know, so that they can prepare their defences. I quite often say to people something like 'if you tell me about that, I shall be obliged to take action on it' or 'now that I've found out about that, I shall have to report it, and you might like to work out what to do about it...'

One example of this that I came across was an officer who was concerned with grant aid for voluntary organisations from a local authority. As a result, he was often asked to sit on committees to advise and help the voluntary organisations. From these contacts he acquired information about the organisations, which eventually came to influence the advice that he gave the local authority committee. This was fine when things were going well, but it soon came to the point when cuts in grant aid had to be made and, inevitably, adverse things that he had learned about the organisations began to count in some of the decisions. Some of the committee members felt that this was disloyal to the committees. So it was. It would have been better to avoid sitting on the committees, to offer advice as a consultant, and then all sides could have controlled the information that was passed around. By getting close to the organisations he helped his local authority masters, while leaving committee members at least uncertain and often suspicious of his motives. In the end, this led to a breakdown in many important relationships, which would have been maintained by more open dealing.

Being open about conflicts of interest can enhance your

reputation for straight dealing with others and help your linking function by bringing you more information and involvement because people learn to trust you.

CONFRONTATION

Occasionally, you have to confront people with problems or difficulties, and this is always an anxious business. Effective confrontation requires clarity about precisely what is wrong and what needs to change and a strategy for raising the problem with the person who needs to do something about it.

Generally, confrontations are best done in private, where the person who is being confronted does not have to keep up appearances in front of anyone else. The best approach is a calm, friendly one of 'we are having a problem about this; can we sort it out together?' Be specific about the problem, and negotiate about the action to be taken; avoid making demands. Always give someone alternatives, rather than backing them into a corner. Try to support them personally, by helping them make decisions and avoiding personal criticism, placing the problem in the 'system' rather than with individuals. Work together to resolve the problem, rather than leaving it to the person being confronted.

Occasionally, confrontation has to be done in an open meeting, for example to gain support from a constituency. In this case, it should be preceded by a warning so that it is not a surprise to the people confronted. You can say things like 'I'm very worried about this and I shall have to raise it at the meeting if it comes up again.' In one example of this, in public meetings that I was chairing, some committee members were criticising staff. I said in general terms that this was not appropriate and should be dealt with in committee or privately. When it happened again, I contradicted the criticisms and congratulated staff in their work; this got a round of applause from the meeting, and made it clear to staff and critics that there was no widespread criticism.

MISTAKES AND DISASTERS

Even the most tactful person puts their foot in it sometimes, but when linking, your organisation's standing may be at risk as well as your own relationships. If contacts between organisations become strained as a result, service to the public may suffer.

If you become aware of having upset or annoyed someone, or think you might have done, instant reaction is often the best course. Go out of your way to say you have realised that you might have caused offence, apologise and offer to do anything which may help to set the matter right. It is very hard for someone to be annoyed with an obviously contrite and embarrassed apologist. Warning someone about something that may rebound on them as a result of what you have done helps them rectify it and defend themselves against any problems.

DEALING WITH COMPLAINTS

Another responsibility which linking people take up occasionally is that of receiving complaints. It is often a difficult task to get the response right.

There are some reactions that should be avoided. First, there are extremes of total acceptance or total rejection of a complaint. Many complainants are not familiar with your organisation and may have their facts wrong or their expectations of or attitude to your organisation may be inappropriate. It is, therefore unwise simply to apologise or accept that the complaint is correct unless you are sure that this is so. This is especially so if it is about another person in the organisation, who may well have a full answer to the complaint. On the other hand, it is offensive to reject the complaint, since the complainant may have a good case.

The best approach in the first instance is to acknowledge the hurt, anger or frustration of the complainant with a few words such as 'I'm sorry your are upset.'

It is then important to try to get a complete understanding of what has happened. This serves two purposes. In the first place, it shows the complainant that they are being taken seriously. Second, and more important, a full understanding of what the complainant feels and what has gone wrong is needed if things are to be put right. It may not be entirely clear why the complaint is being made. Has the complainant not received a service that was expected? Did she/he ask for the service, or merely assume what would happen? Was she/he treated discourteously? Does the complainant want recompense? Or to have the service or a substitute provided? How can you prevent the same thing happening to someone else? Each of these complaints, and others that might be imagined, demand a different form of response to satisfy the complainant. Offering to prevent the same thing happening again will not, for instance, satisfy someone who wants recompense. The detail of what happened is also important. Who did what, when and in what context? If a service was not provided, was it asked for, or were alternatives offered?

The next aspect of dealing with a complaint is to promise to investigate and reply. Before the investigation, it is usually not possible to say what will be done. To avoid committing the organisation, therefore, it is best to say something like 'we'll look into this very carefully and be in touch again.' If possible, a deadline for reply lets people know where they stand, both the complainants and the people complained against.

After this, the matter can be referred to whoever is appropriate to deal with it. If this is uncertain, the most senior member of staff would be the best recourse, or if there are no staff, the chair or secretary of the organisation. If you are not the channel of reply, it is wise to check that something has in fact been done.

Replying to a complaint is a delicate matter, because the wishes and interests of the complainant may well conflict with those of whoever is complained against, and you may have more of a continuing relationship with the person who is the object of the complaint. Whatever the reply, it is important to acknowledge the feelings of the complainant and also possibly those of the person complained against.

Set out clearly what the result of their complaint is and what you have done about it. I always like to explain what happened fairly fully, and show how decisions have been arrived at. This approach can have its problems, however, because complainants can use the additional information from your reply to pursue their complaint at a higher level. I regard this as their right, but I do not find my superiors so enthusiastic about it because they then have more difficulty in fending off an appeal. It may be necessary to find out what sort of detail in a reply is acceptable to your organisation, perhaps by checking the text of your letter with the person responsible.

Sometimes when a complaint has been received, it reveals the fact that the organisation has no clear way of resolving problems and in providing a service or receiving or dealing with complaints. Complaints can be a good way of identifying problems in an organisation, identifying ways in which a service could be improved or staff who need supervision, support or training. It is useful to identify a process for recording complaints, dealing with them and seeing if there are any patterns about which something should be done.

Complaints are sometimes received about individuals who are being cared for, too, and these can be very difficult to handle. An elderly relative or a child might have been cantankerous or argumentative today, and a helper might have said: 'I'm not going to carry on if he's going to be like this.' This places you in a quandary: do you lose the help, or make your relative more cantankerous or argumentative, or take it up with them and find that there was good reason for the way they were? This is the same problem faced by the professional who receives a complaint about their organisation, but in a more personal way.

Complaints, particularly in personal situations, should never be neglected, however. Even the mildest expression of anxiety or difficulty can build up to real problems; yet a minor problem, which can often be sorted out with little trouble in the early stages, may require heavy investment of emotional energy later on. Comments about individuals being cared for, or the situation they are in, which might be complaints should therefore be investigated as carefully as complaints about organisations. Enquire closely about the particular problem, the time it happened, what took place, how it was handled and so on. Then, with the person complained about, ask about the incident and listen to their side of it before making any judgement. Often one or both parties can be helped by advice about the best way to deal with a similar problem, or sympathetic listening about their feelings and supportive comments, such as how you face and deal with the same problems, or clear demonstration of understanding about their feelings.

EXERCISES FOR CHAPTER 7

1 Identifying misinterpretation

A List a number of decisions or information items that have recently affected you or that you have recently had to pass on.

B For each item on your list, identify the relevant audience(s).

C For each audience identify how it might have been misinterpreted, bearing in mind their interests; have a real fantasy.

D For each misinterpretation, identify how it might have been avoided.

2 Practising misinterpretation (for a team)

A Identify a number of pieces of information or decisions that have recently been conveyed to you or your organisation.

B Appoint one person to explain each item, and the others are to receive it and misinterpret it (as avidly as possible). And then take turns to be the information giver.

C Identify ways in which the information giver tried to avoid misunderstandings and correct the misinterpretations.

3 Confrontations

A Identify an important issue for you or your team which can be dealt with by confronting someone else about how they have acted. Identify who specifically should be approached about it.

B Role play the confrontation, first with the target being difficult, and then with them acting co-operative.

C Review and list possible techniques for dealing with confrontation used in the role plays.

4 Likely complaints

A Brainstorm (i.e. working together list rapidly with no evaluation of ideas) all the possible things people could complain about in you, your team, your office or the person you are helping and the situation they are in.

B For each possible complaint, no matter how silly, think of ways in which they could have been prevented.

C Divide up responsibility for sorting them out.

5 Complaints system

A Have you got a complaints system? If not, go to stage E. If you have a system, look at every complaint you have received in the last three months.

B   If you have not received any complaints, or you have no record of any complaints, you need to look at the adequacy of your definition of what a complaint is, your publicity of the availability of the complaints system or the people to whom complaints can be made or your recording system for complaints. Then go to stage E.

C   For every complaint received review it against the system to see if it was dealt with adequately, to assess whether the procedure helped or hindered dealing with the complaint and what the outcomes were. Consider in each case and for each stage of the procedure what went well, what went badly and what could have been done better. Score (from 1 poor to 5 excellent) each stage of the procedure for each complaint on whether the procedure was satisfactory for dealing with the complaint. From your scores and judgements, identify parts of the procedure that work well and badly, and types of complaint for which the procedure works well and badly.

D   If the outcomes in each case resulted in no change of practice or policy, consider whether you have a self-justification system rather than one for complaints.

E   Write or re-write a complaints scheme to follow these stages
   •   general principles
   •   publicising the scheme
   •   receiving and recording the complaint
   •   initial response
   •   investigation of the complaint
   •   final response to the complainant
   •   compensation for the complainant (including statements of intent, recognition of justification etc.)
   •   changes in policy and practice arising form the complaint
   •   recording and reviewing the complaints received and the system.

Eight:
co-ordination

MOVING ON TO STRUCTURED LINKING
THROUGH CO-ORDINATION

So far, we have been examining individual skills in linking activities. Now, we are moving on to look at the way in which those skills may be used to strengthen the effectiveness of linking between organisations and individuals. Obviously, it is possible to go on liaising and representing your organisation and individuals' needs, and this will be required fairly continuously as new situations come up to be dealt with. However, getting organisations and individuals to co-ordinate their activities provides a degree of continuity. This helps to avoid the need for constant liaison work, because it ensures that organisations and individuals working together think the same way and seek the same objectives. So, instead of constantly checking that everything is all right, you can ensure this by making both organisations and groups work in the same direction. Similarly, people working together in the care of an individual can co-ordinate their work so that, by thinking along the same lines, they do not have to expend so much energy in everyday planning for their tasks.

Co-ordination is concerned with ensuring that organisations or individuals who work together consistently do so in ways which fit together. This is different from co-operation. You can be co-operative, in the sense that you are prepared to help another organisation or individual meet their objectives and work together on them; what Warham (1970, p 186) calls 'harmonious and well-planned working relationships between individuals'. This does not necessarily imply being co-ordinated, which Warham defines as 'a structural integration of the services themselves.' At least, co-ordination suggests the planned alignment of your activities. Aiken *et al.* (1975) include co-operation among the three aspects of co-ordination that they identify: that services should be comprehensive, compatible and co-operative.

Co-ordination involves five activities:

- avoiding gaps in services and activities between organisations or individuals;
- avoiding overlaps in services;
- developing aligned strategies in providing services;
- developing aligned attitudes and values;
- developing integrated structures in the services.

The next sections examine these in turn.

AVOIDING GAPS

However well-planned social and community services are (and often they are very little planned), there are bound to be gaps in the provision. This is because the infinite variety of human need always throws up something that organisational structures with boundaries cannot cope with. While at one time many organisations would have stretched a point and taken something on which was on the boundaries of their responsibilities, financial constraints have meant that flexibility is less in evidence in many agencies. If services are to be comprehensive, negotiation or a clear understanding of boundaries between agencies is required; sometimes the appearance of unconsidered needs leads to the formation of new specialist agencies, which then have difficulty gaining a place in service provision.

Another reason why gaps in provision are a more common problem than in the past is the fragmentation of services which has taken place with the growth of government support, in the UK, for private and voluntary sector activities. This is likely to increase in the 1990s as community care, health service and criminal justice policies encourage the formation of smaller organisations and more competition between them.

Gaps may exist between the boundaries of services available at any one time. So, a social services department may have day and residential care provision for elderly people, with day care provision which is unable to deal with someone who is incontinent. Where the client is not otherwise sufficiently in need to go into residential care, but is unable to look after themselves fully because of the incontinence, a gap in the boundaries of services exists, and might be dealt with by the provision, for example, of more domiciliary care or incontinence services from the health authority.

Gaps also exist in timing. For example, if a child is disturbed and difficult in his/her behaviour, special provision might be made at school for the child's supervision, and for transport home. Where there is uncertainty about whether the parents can always be ready to receive the child at home, a gap in arrangements exists leaving a time which needs to be covered. In this case, it might be achieved by special post-school provision, and a negotiation would have to take place about whether this is a responsibility of the education or social services departments or the extent to which it is so. If such a service does not exist, there is also, here, a gap in boundaries of services.

There are a variety of approaches to co-ordination in this situation:

- *Negotiation of boundaries*–this can take place at a general level, so that when a series of problems arise, agencies can negotiate a new arrangement of boundaries between them. Alternatively, it may be done on a case-by-case basis, in which workers or individuals agree who will do what as problems arise. This is usually the most appropriate way of sorting out difficulties in an individual case, where a group of carers are working with one individual or family, and relies on linking work in liaison and representation already discussed earlier in this book. The relative who is undertaking most of the care, or a key worker from an agency, might arrange a meeting of people involved to sort out tasks. Approaching the problem through boundary negotiation sees the services as part of a system, in which the elements of the system are not fitting together well enough. The assumption lying behind this approach is that boundaries between services should normally be aligned, and that individual arrangements are needed when it becomes apparent that this is not so.
- *Pathway negotiation*–in this way of dealing with co-ordination problems, the worker or carer seeks a pathway through the different services from one or the other. Again, agencies may negotiate a series of standard pathways through services down which clients will usually pass. The tariff in criminal justice is rather like this; people start with a caution, progress to conditional discharges, fines, probation, community service, and then custodial sentences. People are seen as progressing through this process, but may speed up,

slow down or fall out of the system altogether. Similarly, elderly people may progress from minimal home help services, to more intensive home care, to day care and then to residential care as their condition deteriorates. Pathways are very rarely straight or consistent, and the implication of many modern services is that pathways which meet particular needs should be carefully worked out on an individual basis. This approach to dealing with gaps does not make the assumption that services will usually have contiguous boundaries, but that gaps will routinely exist, and the task is to steer people between services to find the most appropriate combination. This may become more relevant as services become smaller, more fragmented and less subject to the overall planning of large monopoly providers from the state.

AVOIDING OVERLAPS

Avoiding overlaps presents many similar problems as the task of avoiding gaps; negotiation in some form between providers of services will have to be organised.

However, overlaps present the additional issue of competition and its consequences. Competition implies that the services would both like to provide for a particular individual or group in need. Some people would argue that competition is bad for services as a whole, because it represents a waste of resources. If only one effective service were present, it could provide adequately for needs, and other resources could similarly be applied to other needs on an organised basis. An effective service would be one which adequately met the needs and perhaps also the preferences of all potential clients of it. Competing services, it might be argued, waste resources in providing alternatives which might not be fully used. One planned service does not need to offer alternatives, and so does not waste resources in the same way. Even if services are not fully planned, at least efforts should be made to ensure that services are complementary, so that they add to the full range of provision, rather than overlapping and competing.

This argument does not really stand up to examination. For one thing, clients may have legitimate preferences which might imply that one service is never sufficient. One person's competition is another person's personal preferences. For example, one elderly person being admitted to residential care might prefer to live in the country, another in the town; one might prefer to live near their old home, another near a distant relative. One residential home is unlikely to provide this, although one co-ordinated service might do so. However, it is often the case that co-ordinated services have policies about what is the most desirable way of meeting needs which tend to reject certain aspects of provision and reduce choice. An example is where enthusiasts for 'normalisation' in mental illness services (which implies people living in environments which are as like as possible those valued by people without such a condition) reject the needs for asylum care for some people who might need it occasionally, or residential care where people prefer or need the support of communal living.

Another reason why arguments against competition do not always stand up is that services may provide for similar or related needs while offering fundamentally different alternatives. For example, it is possible to run a residential care home in fairly traditional ways, or as a therapeutic community, thus affording a completely different style of provision which might legitimately be preferable for some clients. Again, it is often the case that one organisation, while it may accept the case for this variety of provision, does not have the management skill to develop the whole range; the management of, say, a traditional residential setting, requires fundamentally different attitudes to care from the management of, say, a therapeutic community.

One point of view against competition is that it is for the benefit of the providers and not the people who use the service. In this view, the reason for alternative provision is the financial advantage of suppliers (if they are profit-making) or to their greater glory (if they are non-profit-making and have a policy or ideology about how they go about their work). The alternatives provided may not then be particularly advantageous to clients.

There are a number of points to be made against this view. First, some clients may actually welcome the element of ideology in a service. For example, there is a long history of special services for people from particular religious denominations, which recognise particular aspects of clients' beliefs. Another example is services which follow a communal ideology, such as the therapeutic community, or make special efforts to undertake services in a way which may be attractive to clients; by relying on community involvement or local volunteers for example. Second, it is possible to be committed to an ideology and recognise that it does not suit everyone, so being prepared to take part in a network of services. Third, all workers in the social services receive payment for their work, and receiving payment through (reasonable) profit or by being able to fulfil one's beliefs is only another form of recognition of one's work. Fourth, even within fairly comprehensive public services, there is competition and conflict between various aspects and personnel in the services; this is often not well-controlled and may be as damaging as competition between independent services and less well-acknowledged. Finally, it is necessary to make the point that it is equally an ideology which believes in comprehensive public services and public duty as the appropriate form of social services, and this approach has its own evils of bureaucracy and inflexibility - these are not particularly advantageous to clients either.

Another argument against competition is the behavioural consequences of it. Thus, where competitive services exist, they may seek to fulfil their own aims without concern for other related services. So, in the residential care and nursing home field, for example, there have been stories of the operators of homes making links with (and even payments to) other professionals, or seeking to persuade clients to use their services when alternatives have not been explored and might be better for them. People in competing services may become personally competitive and spiteful or hostile to one another to the detriment of clients. However, against this tendency can be placed the characteristic of many competitive markets for agencies and individuals to find a niche for their own particular skills where there is little competition, or to come to agreements with others to avoid damaging behaviour. It is not a necessary characteristic of competition that it becomes hostile; indeed it is often negotiated.

There are also practical arguments against the view that competition should always be avoided. Even if you start off with a well-planned system, in which people with different needs are directed to different aspects of the services, their characteristics change as time goes on, and the service changes to meet the changed needs. If older people enter sheltered housing, and then grow more dependent, the tendency is to add to services in the housing, rather than move the client to alternative accommodation. As a result of this tendency working in lots of different places, services with apparently clear boundaries fairly naturally come to overlap in what they are providing.

Responses to competition need to take account of the problems that it often raises and use the advantages and positive aspects of it to the benefit of clients. These responses include the following:

- *Awareness* of the possibility and complexities of competition. Whatever the pattern of services, we are likely to experience competitive feelings and competitive behaviour in the social services. This may be because of jealousy, differing ideologies, thoughtlessness or fear (of financial loss, failure and so on). If we are aware of and look out for such behaviour, we are much less likely to be surprised or thrown by people behaving unreasonably and can raise any issues which arise with them. Equally, we need to be aware of competitive feelings in ourselves.
- *Review of services* where there are boundaries to see where competition and overlap may arise. This can help to identify points where problems are likely to arise.
- *Negotiation* about ways of dealing with clients, of boundaries of services, ways in which clients are to pass from one service to another, and agreement to inform each other about likely conflicts may help to avoid problems.
- *Clarity* about ideological, theoretical and philosophical differences between services may help us to understand frustrations between colleagues and see where clients may be helped by referral to overlapping services.
- Regular *co-ordinating* meetings may help agreed and negotiated boundaries to be maintained.

ALIGNED STRATEGIES

So far, we have been examining events or occasions in which co-ordination may be difficult. However, we have noted that organised links may help to avoid these occasions arising, and agencies may well want to establish shared strategies to agree regular patterns of response to differing approaches to their work. Similarly, individuals working on the problems of a particular person may want to agree strategies for dealing with them.

Co-ordination through aligned strategies may be:

- task-centred;
- person-centred; or
- strategy-centred.

Where the strategy is task-centred, it is around particular services or activities which agencies or a group of workers or helpers do together. Thus, an agreement between police, the probation services, relevant voluntary agencies and social services about how to deal with offenders younger than the age of criminal responsibility would be task-centred, since it is an agreed way of dealing with a shared problem; it is problem-based. An agreement between these agencies on co-operation over the needs of a particular youngster would be person-centred, since co-operation in this instance is organised round the needs of a particular individual. A joint committee to deal with young offenders on a particular council estate would be strategy-centred, since it is an organised plan towards an agreed objective. Strategy-centred alignment is fundamentally issue-based. Within this, task-centred or person-centred approaches might be taken in particular cases.

Negotiating aligned strategies involves:

- identifying agencies or individuals with an interest in the task, person or issue;
- taking responsibility for agreeing the nature of the problem to be dealt with, agreed activities and shared aims;
- agreeing a plan for monitoring the activities;
- agreeing a timescale for reviewing aims and planning again.

DEVELOPING ALIGNED ATTITUDES AND VALUES

Aligning attitudes and values represents a step forward from aligned strategies. It is relatively easy to agree to work together around particular tasks, people or issues where several agencies or individuals have a shared interest. However, in many instances, to do the work successfully requires an agreed approach to the problem.

For example, you may have to work with a headteacher in a school concerning a boy who is frequently playing truant. The approach to the problem may be fundamentally different. The headteacher may start from a position of being punitive and have the objective of ensuring that the boy remains in school. A social worker might start from a position of wanting to enquire into the boy's reasons for absence and have the aim of removing the circumstances which give rise to those reasons, thus inducing the boy's return to school with a positive motivation. In another example, a hospital social worker may be asked to help an elderly woman sort out her affairs with the aim (on the part of the consultant geriatrician) of discharging her as soon as possible. The social worker may well start off from a position of wanting the woman to feel safe and secure about returning home.

In each of these instances, co-ordination of services cannot take place unless the different occupations involved have an agreed philosophy about their aims and means of action. Very often social workers start out trying to deal with a case on the false assumption that there is agreement about why and how action should be taken, and this fails because of the absence of agreement.

To try to align attitudes and values, therefore, you need to:

• explore explanations for the problem we are dealing with;
• explore debates about the reasons for taking action;
• explore the range of actions which might be taken, and pros and cons of each.

This should enable you to identify where there are fundamental disagreements and either come to a view about them, avoid them by not taking action in an area where there is disagreement or fall back on aligning strategies without seeking fuller agreement.

INTEGRATED STRUCTURES

If attitudes and values can be aligned, further co-operation does move towards co-ordination, which involves finding structures so that members of more than one agency, or more than one part of an agency, or several people with different concerns can work regularly together. There are a variety of structures which can facilitate links (Payne, 1982), some of which have already been discussed in this book. They are given here more or less in order of complexity and degree of involvement in the other agency or group:

• *Contact*, where people from one agency or group are appointed to receive contacts from the other group or group.
• *Outreach*, where people from one agency or group are appointed to contact the other as required.
• *Linking*, where people are appointed to receive contacts or to make them at regular intervals.
• *Liaison*, where people are appointed to have regular links and to undertake regular work with members of the other agency or group.
• *Outposting*, where people are placed wholly or partly in the other agency or group and undertake work with the other agency or group. A common way of organising this in or

between agencies is a *matrix* structure, in which one or more members from different parts of an agency or from different agencies work together for a specific project or to carry out shared work for a period.

- *Interfacing*, where people are appointed to be equal members of both agencies or groups.
- *Interleaving*, where people from both groups take on work within the other.
- *Merger*, where both groups undertake all shared work together.

Each of these structures can be used for a particular task or for an area of work, and, while they require a degree of agreement about values and attitudes to start with, may well help shared philosophies to develop and encourage more complex and involving structures to grow. Many agencies or groups of people use shared working as a strategy to strengthen links and build co-operation so that their work is easier in the longer term.

CONCLUSION

The purpose of this chapter has been to emphasise the importance of planning and organising co-ordination to attain consistency in linking activities. By co-ordinating activities between agencies and individuals working with clients, it is possible to have a longer-term security about the links that we have developed in particular cases or to meet specific needs. Co-ordination allows further development of linking to work with a range of cases or problems.

Many of the skills used in making co-ordination work are the individual skills of approaching other agencies and colleagues, planning links with them, understanding and planning your role and strategies in meetings and committees with them. These were examined in the earlier parts of this book. Co-ordination represents a more general application of these skills to broader strategic aims in building links between agencies.

However, attempts to co-ordinate activities rely on a basic level of co-operation and shared aims in the first place, and this is not always possible. Subsequent chapters look at ways of dealing with the need to build up this initial level of co-operation. The next chapter looks at building coalitions with others in order to influence people in power, or to have an impact on a problem which seems intractable with the resources available to you.

EXERCISES FOR CHAPTER 8

1 Considering needs for co-ordination
A List every organisation with which you work regularly on projects or with clients, and where work will be continuing.
B For each organisation, list difficulties which have been experienced in that work in the last six months.
C For each difficulty, analyse whether the difficulty arose because of problems in relationships between
  • personnel
  • attitudes and values
  • aims and objectives
  • timing
  • use of resources.
D For each of these analyse whether one of the five co-ordination strategies would help overcome the difficulties.

2 Planning co-ordination
A Identify a situation where co-ordination seems useful.
B Draw a map of the people involved, their attitudes, aims and resources.
C From the material in the map, draw a force-field analysis of the things which are positively pushing you towards co-ordination and those restraining you (including attitudes and personal problems).

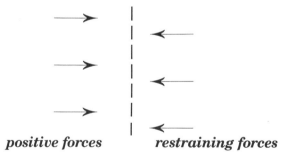

positive forces   *restraining forces*

D Attempt the same analysis from the point of view of the other party or parties.

3 Approaching co-ordination
A Identify an issue requiring co-ordination, and carry out the analysis in Exercise 2.
B Use this as a briefing for a role play of both sides coming to an agreement about a co-ordination structure. Use the analysis of different kinds of co-ordinating structure worked out above.

Nine:
advocacy, alliance and coalitions

THE IMPORTANCE OF CREATING ALLIANCES

Much social work is individual, and, of course, helping people meet their special needs is very much a matter of responding to them as individuals. Similarly, much support and management of social workers is carried out individually, through personal supervision and mutual help and consultation. This often leads to social workers operating individualistically. Even when co-operating with others and building links, this is treated as a personal thing, perhaps done on behalf of a team and a group. Carers for people in the community also see their work very much as a matter of personal loyalty and responsibility. Much of what we have so far examined in this book has been about the personal use of skills on behalf of others.

In many cases, however, the individualistic approach is not enough to achieve the best possible results on behalf of clients. As this approach is so ingrained or natural to the sort of work most social workers and carers do, they often neglect the possibilities for developing support for their work and their clients' needs through alliances and coalitions. This activity has been well-developed in community work and in social action and campaigns for social and political objectives. Many people in the community can cultivate the necessary skills for themselves (see for example, Wilson, 1986). One reason why social workers neglect it may be its association with political action which, for many social workers in official positions and carers with personal responsibilities, may seem to be irrelevant or impossible to implement.

Many of the skills and strategies developed in community work and social action can be used on the smaller scene of social care, both within organisations in which social workers are employed and to influence other organisations or individuals on behalf of clients.

THE ROLE OF ADVOCACY

Another aspect of acting on behalf of clients and people we care for is the developing field of advocacy. Originally, this was seen as a form of individual representation by experts on behalf of people who were unable to speak for themselves, or did not have sufficient expertise in procedures. The original model is that of a lawyer acting as an advocate in court. For many years, it has been regarded as an integral part of social work that social workers should act as advocates for their clients within official systems or where there were difficulties in getting their voice heard. This is known as *case advocacy*.

Another form of advocacy, developed in the 1970s, builds up information from individual cases to promote social change for the benefit of groups of clients. This *cause advocacy* is concerned with identifying and promoting certain social causes.

In the 1980s, these approaches broadened still further towards a concept of *citizen advocacy* (Butler *et al.*, 1988). This developed from work in the field of people with learning difficulties, in which an independent volunteer built up a trusting relationship with a person who was unable to speak for themselves, and represented their need in the powerful decision-making processes in hospitals and other agencies. The concept has extended to other clients groups, particularly people with handicaps and those recovering from mental illness. It has also been used on behalf of children in care. Building on the learning gained through working with the advocate, advocacy groups have developed so that people can give each other mutual support to seek change for their own needs. *Self-advocacy* of this kind thus comes to be connected with alliance- and coalition-building generally, and increasingly social workers are asked to help such groups or feel the need to encourage them to develop as part of their work.

Such approaches offer an important way of empowering clients to act on their own behalf. An essential aspect of effective empowerment for a group with social needs is promoting alliances between individuals, so that mutual support enables them to use and strengthen their own personal power, and overcome the factors in their lives and, perhaps, early maturation which have led to the loss of personal power.

BUILDING ALLIANCES

The first step in building alliances on behalf of clients or people you care for is to examine carefully the particular issue that you want to deal with. There is a tendency to feel that the entire life situation of a person should be dealt with as a whole, but it is hard to get support and involvement in everything at once. Even when dealing with an individual, helpers and supporters, as opposed to the closest full-time carer, cannot usually be involved in everything - their help needs greater focus. This is even more true when dealing with a group of clients and trying to gain support from possibly interested people and agencies who, nonetheless, will have many other interests and commitments. Defining and clarifying the issue to be worked on is crucial. It is important, so far as possible, to make the issue a positive one - you want to achieve something. In some ways, it is easier to create a *defensive* alliance (to stop something happening) because all that is needed it to put up enough obstructions. However, this will often not prevent a really determined or powerful bureaucracy or organisation from doing what it wants, particularly if it is not responsive to public pressure. It is usually better to seek a positive alternative, and this is more encouraging to people who might want to join you.

The second step is to identify likely supporters. These may be people working in a similar field or with similar interests. Alternatively, it may be possible to identify supporters who might have an interest in the resolution of an issue for their own convenience. For example, I was once involved in working with a group of colleagues to change the system for dealing with rent arrears, a system that was making it difficult for clients to manage their affairs. We started out by thinking that colleagues in the housing department would oppose this, because we assumed that the bureaucratic pressures on them and their view of the world would prevent them from taking our point of view. We saw them, through the occasional contacts we had, as having a very simple justice model of rights and wrongs in paying rent. In fact, they turned out to have a considerable interest in removing a problem that caused them a lot of hassle. We also discovered that they were sympathetic to the needs of tenants and saw their role as helping to resolve their problems; however, they also saw more clearly than we did the long-term consequences of not paying rent, both for the tenant and for the credibility of the housing department. In identifying supporters therefore, it is useful to review the range of organisations and individuals who have connections with the issue. I always try to start out by assuming that others will be sympathetic to people in difficulties, even if their jobs make it difficult for them to act on their feelings. Not only is this a more positive way of viewing the world, which keeps up my morale, it is more likely to appeal to possible allies and more likely to gain their support.

The sort of motivations which many people have, according to Dluhy (1990), are:

- ideological or personal beliefs;
- some tangible benefit for the person;
- tangible benefits for the person's agency or family;
- social involvement (for example, getting to know people in the field);
- improving their standing in their agency or the community;
- ability to gain more information, knowledge and skills;
- ability to improve their own situation or that of their clients or the people they are caring for;
- a feeling of duty and responsibility.

The next move is to make contact with potential supporters and gain their interest in finding a solution to the issue which you have raised. It may well be necessary to use many of the personal skills discussed in other chapters to engage their interests and commitment. Often, a useful approach will be to hold a meeting - either formal or informal - to work out action which can be taken.

One of the important features of building commitment to an alliance is not to try to take over too much of the thinking and action yourself (or conversely, to rely too much on someone else). If people are to give their commitment, this can most strongly be engaged by involving them in having the ideas and working out a plan of campaign. It is important to involve everyone, avoid elitism or cliques, be open about reasons for involvement and make sure those who take part in important activities are representative of the interests of all the members of the alliance.

As the alliance builds, you will need jointly to explore the extent of the problem and jointly to define it carefully. Then, exploration of various options for action will follow fairly naturally. These options may include the following:

- Informing people (especially those with power or influence over the outcome) of the issue and its consequences.
- Undertaking and promoting research so that the problem can be more fully understood.
- Identifying people with an interest or influence in having the issue resolved.
- Listening to their responses to the problem and especially the objections they put up to your proposed solutions - this may

give you clues about what is preventing action in the direction you are proposing, and help you to identify ways of overcoming the obstructions.

- Trying to get the issue and your solutions to it onto formal agendas of individuals and organisations who can do something about it.
- Gaining support, and expressions of the difficulties from clients and other people affected.
- Generating ideas for positive practical action to resolve the difficulty. It is usually not too effective to just complain or present a problem - it usually works far better to have a clear proposal for its resolution.
- The most important aspect of the problem is to present an image of it in such a way that people want to do something about it; constructing the right image of the problem and your alliance (both positive and persistent) is essential. One angle of this is looking to see why people might *not* want to do anything about the problem - what are the things which stop people wanting to take action about the problem? It may be something in the nature of the problem (for example, people tend to be hostile to causes which they see as undeserving) or something about your alliance (for example, you are relatively powerless people, or you have a self-interest which can be seen as returning an unfair personal dividend to you).
- You may have to apply various forms of pressure to achieve change; these are dealt with in Chapter 14 on 'Lobbying'.
- One of the most important moves is to identify influential people who make the decisions or influence aspects of the problem, and it is these who need to be targeted for your approach and persuasive efforts.
- When you are successful (and even if you are not), thank people for their involvement, and perhaps have social events to maintain their spirits, support and involvement, even it this is just a cup of coffee or a drink in the pub. This ensures that people are more prepared to come back to you over another issue, and gives them a personal as well as professional or community interest in involvement.

In the average attempt to influence your own organisation or another bureaucracy, the sort of approach you will use will often be through writing letters, reports and through various meetings. You may have to take several steps, such as building up a liaison system in order to gain influence to have an issue resolved. Generally, if you are working alongside people in other agencies, or already have a formal liaison system set up, they will be far more inclined to respond to your requests for change.

One such group that I was involved with was a group of professionals working on a council estate; membership included local priests, health authority staff, housing department staff, social services and probation officers, together with representatives of local voluntary agencies. We co-ordinated pressure on each of our agencies for more resources and, because we came to know each other well, were able to support, at the ground level in different agencies, proposals for co-operation from other agencies which might otherwise have fallen on stony ground. The fact that we appeared to be doing a good job of co-operation seemed to give the group more status, so that there was greater awareness in the senior managements of the agencies of the needs of the area. Feedback on how helpful one agency had been to another resulted in a much more positive attitude to workers from management in the latter agency because they were getting good feedback about the work.

Another group of which I am currently a member is a local residents' group working on environmental issues. This group contains no professionals, except a retired estate agent with experience of planning issues, and we have no official status. But our consistent attendance at local planning meetings has led to informal consultations from planning staff. We have also regularly replied to public notices and always present a carefully argued case whenever we make points, so that officials have become used to dealing with us and receiving helpful information and co-operation from us.

It is evident, therefore, that more extensive means of influence may prove unnecessary. People from the community may often use similar techniques, but may also have to use a campaigning style which is beyond the bounds of this book.

One useful technique, both for building alliances and coalitions and for gaining influence, is the use of publications. Many larger and longer-lasting groups produce a small newsletter or series of pamphlets setting out their views, news about people involved, news of developments and accounts of the problems that they are concerned with and ways of dealing with it. This helps to cement the alliance and can also be used as the basis for influencing others.

Another useful thing to try to organise is success. Obviously easy results will not be expected, otherwise you would not have gone to the trouble of building an alliance. Nonetheless, it is useful to identify the tasks you want to undertake in a series of stages, some of the early ones of which you have a good chance of achieving. Another possibility is to include some process objectives within your targets; that is, some targets for getting things done which you hope will have some effect, but do not necessarily rely on others' responses. This might include setting up a committee or publishing a pamphlet or leaflet, carrying out a piece of research or writing a report. You know that with effort you can achieve these, so that you can have some success along the way, even though these particular things may not achieve the change you want to see.

Even though the group you are working with may be relatively informal, it is useful to identify particular responsibilities within it and set clear targets for people. This helps us all get jobs done. The sorts of responsibilities which are important, according to a set of categories adapted from Dluhy and Kravitz (1990), are:

- thinking about the long-term and overall objectives;
- working on finding, keeping and encouraging members;
- keeping up communications between members and from the alliance to others;
- having someone responsible for each special event or activity you organise;
- monitoring the problem, doing research and keeping an eye on changes which take place;
- getting publicity for your aims and work.

All these can be adapted to a fairly wide-scale campaign, an internal piece of lobbying within an agency or a fairly low-key attempt from a group of carers to influence a piece of policy which affects them. Similarly, such approaches can be useful for individuals or groups involved in advocacy.

CONCLUSION

The purpose of this chapter has been to emphasise the importance of building alliances in order to gain mutual support in seeking various objectives for change in services. I have emphasised the value of taking care that the alliance is involving and participative for members, of collecting and using information and research to back up your arguments and, yet again, of having a clear plan and strategy. It is important to be positive rather than negative and help people whom you are seeking to change to respond. Informal and courteous networks of links will help you to achieve change more effectively than public embarrassment and aggression.

EXERCISES FOR CHAPTER 9

1   Assessing support

A   Identify a change that you want to make.

B   List agencies and individuals who might be interested in the change and identify their likely attitudes to the change you want to see.

C   For each individual or agency who is likely to be opposed, identify arguments and approaches to the problem which might convince them to become involved in an alliance.

2   Planning an alliance

A   List the people to be involved in an alliance and identify the issue to be covered.

B   Break down the steps towards achieving the objective, who would be involved in each step and ways of encouraging and motivating their involvement.

Ten:
representative roles

UNDERSTANDING REPRESENTATIVE ROLES

So far, we have been looking at the personal skills required for liaison work, and developing these to create better co-ordination, thus making our work more effective with less continuing liaison effort. The latter parts of the book are concerned with linking skills which are needed to represent people or organisations more actively. If, as we saw in the last chapter, effective liaison and co-ordinating requires working with and creating other organisations, we must also understand and use our roles as representatives of individuals or organisations.

Many people who represent their agency (or their own needs or the needs of a relative, friend or someone they are caring for) take up the task without thinking clearly what role they are supposed to be fulfilling. Knowing what your role is, however, has important advantages.

First, you can identify exactly whom or what you acting for, and how much authority you have. Being clear about this also enables you to check your understanding of the situation with other people who are involved. Second, you can check with yourself whether or how your actions fit in with your role. This helps to reduce the doubt and isolation which often assails us when we are on our own trying to represent something in a hostile or uncaring world.

A role is a set of expectations held about a person occupying a position in a social structure. Expectations are what people think you will do in particular circumstances. They may be about you as a person or about the position you occupy. So, if you are known as being a particularly calm and positive person, people may expect you to be helpful in a crisis. On the other hand, if they know your job is to stick up for people with handicaps, when the crisis involves a reduction in a budget for services for handicapped people, they may not expect you to be particularly calm and supportive to attempts to cut services. This is an example of a situation in which expectations about the same person conflict; your person and your position may be in opposition here.

Expectations which set your role may be your own or those held by other people and, again, their expectations may not be the same as yours.

So, it is not possible to say 'my role is such-and-such.' You have to say what sort of expectations are involved and whose expectations you are talking about when you identify a role.

FOUR COMMON REPRESENTATIVE ROLES

In spite of the complexity of deciding what roles are, there are four common role positions (outlined in Rice, 1965) which can help you to say what your authority and interests are when you are a representative - nominee, representative, delegate/advocate and observer/information gatherer.

Nominee

When representing *organisations* in this role, you are nominated by organisation A to organisation B on the understanding that your allegiance and responsibility is mainly to organisation B. The advantage A gets from this is the opportunity to have someone known to them or having a point of view which is sympathetic to their interests on the inside of organisation B. A common example is where one organisation has power to appoint members to the management or advisory committee of another.

When representing *individuals*, the nominee role is where you act in general for the benefit of the individual A, but pursue activities which do not necessarily concern the individual directly. Again the advantage to A is that you are likely to act in their interests even if you are actually doing something else. For example, long-term carers for housebound elderly people often form support groups. These provide some practical services for the elderly person, but their main purpose is to provide support for the carer and perhaps to seek policy changes and service development. These aims are more general than direct benefit for individual clients but are nonetheless in the longer-term interests of clients with those problems.

I find this point useful for understanding the connection between the specific needs of a client and the broader things that a social worker or other caring person does which are related to but separate from the individual client's needs. If we think of ourselves as the client's nominee prosecuting their interests in the wider world, the connection between our specific and general activities becomes clearer.

Representative

The technical meaning of representative (I have been using the term rather loosely elsewhere) is someone who acts for organisation or individual A to organisation or individual B, and is given general objectives but has the freedom to interpret and act to attain them in their own way. As a representative, you can alter the objectives or anything designed to attain the objectives. You can only do this, however, if the change does not offend against the basic principles and aims of organisation or individual A in having representation with organisation or individual B. This leaves the representative free to negotiate anything provided they adhere to the basic aims, which are set by or agreed with organisation or individual A in the first place.

One of the difficulties with this sort of role is where you think you have freedom to act, and your organisation or the person being represented thinks you should not have taken a particular action which it (or more likely which a group within the organisation) disagrees with. You can prevent this happening by carefully defining the limits of what you can and cannot do in advance. Some sort of clash like this is almost inevitable, however, and you just have to work through it. It helps to have a clear idea of why you are taking actions on behalf of others, and to be able to outline the benefits of your actions.

Delegate/advocate

You are a delegate when you act for organisation or individual A with organisation or individual B in accordance with instructions or an agreement about the aims and activities that you must pursue. If a change of plan is needed, you have to go back for further instructions. While this system is very inflexible, it has the advantage that involvement in decision-making is maintained. So, it is often the basis of advocacy on behalf of clients, in order to demonstrate clearly that they are in control of what is said or done on their behalf.

Being a delegate sometimes has tactical advantages in a negotiation, particularly if there is a lot of conflict involved. You can always say (especially if the other side does not know quite what authority you have) 'I must go back to my people to get a decision.' This can get you out of tight spots, take the pressure off for a while and allow you to think. You may also benefit from psychological backing for your position from whoever you are representing.

Observer/information gatherer

As an observer, you act for organisation or individual A by being present at some event or activity and reporting what happens. You may not be allowed to say anything that matters in the subject or activity that you are observing. Alternatively, one experienced representative I know used to say that he took every opportunity to make 'observations' to another organisation, according to our policy. This was not an active attempt at representation, just a way of keeping the other side well informed. This role is often a useful preparation for further activities. Information is collected which the organisation or individual that you represent can use to form a view or instructions for another role to be taken up. If you are going to apply for a grant from the local authority, for example, or try to affect a health authority's policy, and their meetings are held in public, it may be useful to attend some meetings of the committee which is dealing with your work, to identify personalities who are important, the sort of decisions that are made and their principles or approaches to issues that concern you.

Frequently, these roles are used in conjunction with one another, or one after the other, so that it is possible to analyse a complex set of functions in terms of each role, and still retain some clarity about one's aims and authority.

An example of this is a local MIND (an organisation concerned with mental health issues) group who want to develop volunteer support groups for their housing schemes in the community. They decide to take up an offer to nominate one of their members to the committee of a new volunteer Bureau being set up in the town. The Bureau's aim is to gather a number of experienced committee members for the new Bureau. The representative's general experience of committee work and social services is welcomed, because it gives the Bureau greater credibility. The committee member's responsibility is clearly now for the Bureau. This is a *nominee* role. However, the MIND group gains the advantage that someone with knowledge of and interest in their field is helping to steer the new Bureau, so that it is less likely to do things which are against their interests, and more likely to set up a service which will help them.

The committee member, being competent, is asked to represent the Bureau at a meeting with local authority staff from the social services department about arrangements for a new grant to support their activities. It is agreed that while three posts are being applied for, two will be acceptable provided the salary scales are adequate. The committee members sent to the meeting are left to argue out the points as best they can, bearing in mind the known wishes of the bureau committee. This is a *representative* role.

The discussion hits some snags, and the matter is referred back to the social services committee which meets in public. The MIND nominee is asked to attend and listen to the debate, reporting back on any matters which give clues about the sorts of arguments which will help their case. This is an *observer* role.

Finally, a further meeting with the local authority officers is arranged, and this time the Bureau committee members present are asked to put forward a particular point of view, press for it to be accepted and agree to no other. This is a *delegate* role.

All these examples are typical of the situations which people meet when working in community activities. They equally well apply to individual work for clients. For example, a social worker is working with an occupational therapist to help an elderly man whose legs have been amputated as a result of circulation difficulties. The man lives with a middle-aged daughter and her family. It is agreed that the daughter will collect the man's pension (a nominee role), the occupational therapist will collect information on suitable aids and adaptations available for the man and his family to consider (information gathering). The social worker takes responsibility for checking and arguing for improved social security benefits in whatever way seems most appropriate (representative). The family decide that a particular range of aids and adaptations will be most suitable for their needs, and agree with the occupational therapist and social worker a plan for various ways of obtaining these, so that what is provided is exactly according to their expressed wishes (delegation).

There may be variations in these roles. For example, observers may be asked to be pleasant to the people they are observing or to be strictly neutral in their behaviour. This implies a form of representation, since you are communicating an attitude or policy towards the other group. Another common example is to be a representative in most matters, but to be delegated to act in a particular way over a defined issue. In this situation, where people have got used to you in one role, it is useful to explain what is happening.

Another important point is to see how roles change over time (this again emphasises the importance of understanding timescale in linking work - see Chapter 2). Roles also interlock with one another and are shared between the people involved. If a linking activity is to work properly, particularly if several people are working together on one issue or with responsibility for the needs of one client, clarity about roles is essential. Roles and understanding of them will need to be constantly reconsidered, so that the clarity is continued throughout the time in which responsibility is being shared.

CONCLUSION

The aim of this chapter has been to show how it is possible to analyse roles in linking work, so that activity and responsibility can be clarified, and in particular so that clients and participants in community services can keep control of what is being done on their behalf. In community care services especially, clear delineation of roles in organising a package of care for individual clients is crucial if the package is to be well co-ordinated.

EXERCISE FOR CHAPTER 10

Assessing linking roles

A   Select one individual case and/or one situation in which you are linking with another organisation. Identify the people involved in linking in these situations.

B   For each person involved identify all the different roles undertaken, and show how they relate to one another:
i. by different roles being undertaken in one part of the situation and
ii. by the succession of roles in the situation undertaken by different people or successively by the same person.

C   Identify the points at which roles changed over time, and show how the people involved could have organised their participation so that the changes were specified.

Eleven:
being effective in committee

COMMITTEE WORK IS IMPORTANT

Many people go along to the committee meetings that they must attend without thinking about the best ways of having influence with the members of the committee, or of having an effect on its decisions. This does not make the best use of the opportunity for influencing another organisation or individual.

Similarly, if you are an individual carer working on behalf of a relative and friend, you may want to use involvement on committees to look after your interests or those of the person for whom you are caring. Being effective in committee can be just as important for the individual carer as for a professional.

COMMITTEE PROCEDURE

Most committees are fairly informal, and you should not insist on a more structured procedure merely for the sake of form. It is often possible to make suggestions, discuss them and arrive at decisions without worrying too much about formal procedure.

The person who takes the chair is responsible, on behalf of the members, for conducting the meeting. This requires raising each item on the agenda, encouraging appropriate discussion on it, avoiding inappropriate discussion, helping to cover the topic fully, drawing all the various opinions together and ensuring that a decision is made. Even though this is an important leadership role, each member of the committee has a responsibility to ensure that all the points are covered; the role of the chair does not take that away from everyone else. If there is no formal chair, you all have responsibility for the conduct of the meeting, and should raise issues that worry you about how the meeting is being organised.

The secretary keeps the organisation's records and those of the meeting and acts on behalf of the committee to ensure that things get done. Again, this does not exclude members of the committee from doing things on behalf of it; indeed this is often the main point of having people on the committee. Having a secretary also does not absolve you from keeping your own notes for your own purposes, which may be different from the needs of the meeting. Again, very informal meetings may not need a secretary, and people can take on jobs as required. In some committees jobs are divided up to share the load.

The treasurer keeps records of income and expenditure (or supervises this) so maintaining a check on the financial situation and advises on whether there is enough money for proposed activities. This includes looking ahead to ensure that money will be available in the future. Any major decisions will need to involve the treasurer and gain his/her approval if the committee is to continue to enjoy the confidence and security of ensuring that its finances are healthy. Again, this does not absolve members of the committee from having the responsibility to look at and take a concern for the finances. In informal groups you may not want to worry too much about the formalities, but it is easy to have serious arguments about money and a formal system is best if there is any more to be done than having a contribution for refreshments.

Other members may have particular jobs, represent particular interests or have particular advice or skills to offer. When you join a committee it is useful to find out what people's roles are and what resources they offer to the organisation.

At meetings, there are conventions about behaviour. Generally, only one person should speak at any one time, and people should be polite and tolerant of the views and role of others. Good practice is to support people in carrying out their roles, unless there is concern about how they are doing so, or unless they specifically ask for guidance.

If relationships are strained or there are serious disagreements or difficult or complicated issues to be resolved, it is necessary to proceed more carefully. In this case, the rules of committee procedure are designed to help committees to be fair to all their members and to come to clear decisions. If you do a lot of committee work, therefore, or are part of contentious committees, it is worth studying one of the guides to such procedures mentioned in the list of further reading at the end of this publication (Clarke, 1986; Peel, 1988; Ward, 1985).

Careful preparation of your own views and discussion with leaders, staff and other committee members is an essential part of being successful in committee. It is important to understand the agenda and procedures of the committee to ensure that you can raise matters, have them dealt with, and have minutes which allow you to check on the results of decisions. A stance of lively questioning and contribution to a co-operative endeavour will be helpful. If you behave positively and supportively, demonstrating a commitment, you will have influence even if there is disagreement along the way. Critical involvement is helpful to your host organisation, and to your task in representing someone else.

Agenda

The first necessity is that you have access to an agenda - a list of topics to be discussed at a meeting - and relevant background papers in advance, so that you know what is likely to arise at the meeting you are to attend. Then you can consult others about the topics on the agenda, work out your views, check your own organisation's view and gain support for anything controversial that you may need to put forward.

It is also worth finding out how to have items put on the agenda. Normally, the agenda is specifically planned, but there may be other approaches:

- A standard agenda, so that the same things are discussed at each meeting. The problem with this agenda is that the particular aspects of the topic to be covered will not be apparent.
- Working out the agenda at the beginning of the meeting. The problem with this is that some topics may be pushed out, and discussion may be unprepared.
- Not having an agenda at all. This leads to uncertainty, lack of preparation, and perhaps too much control by the person who takes the chair.
- The agenda is prepared by only one person (often the person in the chair or the secretary) and there is no consultation about what goes into it.

In each case, it is worth trying to persuade the meeting to have an advance agenda which reflects the actual subjects for discussion. It makes the meeting easier to chair, there is greater certainty, better preparation and minutes are easier to take. Also, members of meetings should have the chance to put matters on the agenda; this is an essential aspect of representing someone effectively. Usually, there is a procedure for putting matters up for the agenda, or at least it is possible to find out who creates that agenda and approach them to include something of concern to you.

It can be a helpful strategy to put the matter that you want to raise in writing to the secretary, spelling out any proposal that you want to make, or suggesting a form of words for the agenda. If the matter is complicated or you want to prepare the way for your arguments, you will help your cause by offering to write a paper to go with the agenda, containing background information or a statement of your views. This allows people to be better prepared. This approach is often welcomed, and will be more so if you produce a typewritten version for photocopying, or better still, the requisite number of copies.

It is possible to raise something as 'any other business' (which usually comes at the end of the meeting). This is unwise, since minuting of 'any other business' can be erratic, so discussion or decisions are lost. Also, the person in the chair may exclude matters raised there, so that they are lost or delayed by being put on the agenda of the next meeting because they are too important to be considered without notice. However, if all else fails this may be a useful strategy to get an item onto an agenda, since other members of the committee may support its inclusion in the next meeting's agenda. Careful strategists who are forced into this ploy will ensure, in advance, that they get the support necessary to do this.

Minutes

Minutes are the record of the decisions, and sometimes also the discussions, of a committee. They are usually produced by an appointed secretary. The importance of minutes and how they are worded derives from the fact that they have the final say about what was decided. Ideally, they should be circulated in photocopied or duplicated form, so that each member has their own record. At the next meeting, they should be approved, so that all the committee members can say that they are a correct account of what was agreed. If you think that something you said was not recorded properly or if a decision was not recorded as you thought it should be, you can ask for it to be changed at this point. This sometimes allows you to alter the impact of what you said at the previous meeting.

The only real necessity is for minutes to record what was finally agreed, but it is usual for them also to record any formal procedures, such as a proposal to do something (sometimes called a motion, because it is a suggestion to 'move' the committee in a particular direction; technically, a 'motion' becomes a 'resolution' when it is approved or 'resolved', but some people wrongly use these terms interchangeably). Usually, if there is a vote, the minutes show the voting figures. You can ask for comments to be included in the minutes if you think the comments are important, for example a point in the argument which was particularly crucial or a piece of information. You can also ask that your support for your disagreement with the motion is included. This can be important if you think it was improper or illegal, or against the interests of the people you represent. Asking for your dissent to be recorded emphasises your disagreement and shows to the people you represent that you did your best for them.

Minutes are also important because they allow you to keep a check on whether decisions are implemented and to get reports on things that have happened or been mentioned in the past. There is usually an item called 'matters arising from the minutes' (of the previous meeting) to allow you to ask questions, or for people to report on what has happened since. Some minutes have an 'action list' attached to them (often column against each minute) showing what is to be done and who is to do it. This makes checking what has happened much easier, and is also a good reminder for you.

Raising issues

At the committee, most issues are raised in the normal course of events. However, sometimes, you have the difficult task of raising something which has not arisen from the formal work of the committee. You may wish to raise:

- something you have found out about or thought of;
- something you disagree with;
- something you wish to support or commend to the committee;
- something that has not been raised but which you think should have been.

Raising matters is what you are there for, but if you are mainly representing another body, or an individual who might have a special interest, or if you yourself are seen as having a particular interest, there may be difficulties. Committees are often controlled by the person in the chair, or the secretary, or a staff member, and these people find it threatening if committee members are constantly bringing forward new topics. It may also disrupt everyday business which has to be.

It is often useful, therefore, to test out new material on important members of the committee in private before raising it at the meeting. Perhaps your issue will gain greater influence and support if it is brought forward by leaders in the committee. At the least, they will be prepared for your raising the issue even if they dislike your doing so. You may wish also to gain support from other members of the committee who are likely to be on your side, or interested in what you have to say; advance notice or discussion with them can also help.

You should always test things out in this way if you have to be critical of individuals or of some action which has been taken or is proposed. It can take a lot of emotion out of conflicts if you raise problems privately in advance in a spirit of 'I don't know what the answer is - let's see if we can work it out together.' You are then raising questions so that all concerned can understand better rather than being on the outside criticising those who (maybe) are doing their best. They may have a full answer, in which case it would be wrong to criticise and make a fuss (and it might dent your credibility). If, having talked it over, you still disagree, at least those criticised can feel that you have treated them courteously.

If your point is accepted and some action proposed to deal with it, all well and good. It is useful to think out in advance what you would like to see happen, in case you are asked to suggest an alternative course of action.

You should check that the matter is minuted, by asking for this at the time and checking and, if necessary, amending the minutes at the next meeting.

Sometimes your point will not be accepted and you will have to decide whether to retire gracefully (insisting that the matter is minuted so that you cannot be held responsible for not having raised it at some time in the future), or to press the matter by disagreeing, raising an alternative proposal of your own, putting a critical motion or, in the last resort, resigning.

Asking questions

Asking questions is often an aspect of raising issues, and is also a legitimate part of being a committee member. It may be a tactful way of raising issues. The purpose may be to test out the proposals of those active in the organisation, or the work of staff, or to seek information and explanation of something that has happened. If the matter is complex or requires information to be gathered, you should give notice of the question. You may have to consider that the cost of getting the information together might outweigh the value of having the matter explored.

Questions that you want to raise can always be phrased in such a manner that you are 'testing out' rather than criticising. At times, however, you have to make it clear that the questions you are raising are important to you, and to explain why they are important; perhaps also you can show why they might be important to the host organisation.

Disagreeing

Even disagreeing can be done in a spirit of co-operative endeavour to find the right answer. Some people disagree by pretending to play the devil's advocate (this is a person who puts the contrary view whether they believe it or not so that all the arguments on several sides of an issue are brought out). This can be dishonest and confusing, though, since sooner or later if you are going to press the point you will have to come out into the open with your view. Playing devil's advocate should only be by agreement in order to explore issues fully.

An appropriate approach is sometimes: 'I'm not sure I agree with this - there are several points against it', quietly and unemotionally setting out the arguments and facts clearly. This approach serves well for most ordinary matters. At times, however, a major issue of principle arises for you and conveying the emotive nature of the issue with a little passion (but not such as to seem irrational, patronising or incoherent) helps the case.

When you are disagreeing, it is important to be clear as to what you are aiming for. The aims might be:

- to *stop* what is proposed;
- to attach *conditions* before it goes ahead;
- to *substitute* an alternative proposal; or
- to *clarify* objections and difficulties, or possible pitfalls, so that planning for action may be more effective.

Stopping is sometimes seen as destructive. Very often, something will have to be done anyway, so it is usually best to offer an alternative, or to set conditions or settle for a compromise if your favoured alternative does not win. It may be easier to succeed if, having failed in private to get the leadership or staff on your side, you try out your ideas on a few other committee members, both to see whether there will be support and to see how much compromise is needed. Sometimes members will agree to support you in private, but may only do so in a limited way (e.g. by not attacking you, by speaking for you but not voting for you). Many people dislike making a fuss and will 'keep quiet' whatever they think. They may not like to oppose certain groups, for instance, or they may dislike conflict or wish to avoid upsetting the apple-cart if they have something to raise which is important to them. Other people will prefer to support the organisation and the leadership in general, even though in this particular instance they may disagree with the proposal.

Although disagreeing is a difficult thing to do, it is always much easier if you have a record of supporting the organisation, and giving praise where it is due. Taking every opportunity in a committee to say 'well done' or comment on progress or good points will make others think you are a positive person. They will give much greater credence to your misgivings and accept occasional conflicts or difficulties from you if they feel you are a supporter.

COMMITTEE MEMBERS' RESPONSIBILITIES

The formal responsibilities of a committee member should always be borne in mind. There is a duty to ensure that proper advice (e.g. legal, accountancy, medical) is taken and considered fully, that the constitution and objects of the organisation are complied with and that the procedures established comply with the law (e.g. employment law, accounting practice, company law, inspection regulations for registered residential care homes). Whenever these matters arise, if you do not act properly, you may be held liable for negligence or some illegal act (and so may the organisation which nominated you). This is also the case even if you are the member of the committee (technically the Board of Directors) of a limited liability company. Many voluntary and community organisations are setting themselves up as limited companies to restrict the financial liability of their committee members. They usually become companies limited by guarantee. However, liability is only limited if you behave legally. If you are negligent, you are liable for your negligence. When you are on a committee do not be lulled into a false sense of security that limited liability means no liability.

In this case you want to ensure that the committee acts properly by, for example, obtaining appropriate advice before acting. If others disagree, you should insist on having your dissent from their decision recorded in the minutes, so that you (and your nominating organisation) are not held liable if there is trouble. You may also have to consider whether you should take some other action (e.g. in the courts, by reporting to whoever funds that organisation) to prevent something illegal taking place. In this case, you may need legal advice.

CONCLUSION

This chapter has been concerned to set out the main implications of membership of a committee. The main aspects of formal committee procedure and the main officers have been reviewed. I have emphasised that these are not always necessary in relatively informal groups. Indeed, some people get very irritated by others who insist on excessive formalism. However, formal or informal, members still carry the responsibility among them for making the committee work. In looking at the formal responsibilities of committee members, I pointed out the duty to behave with care, and that this is not excluded by formal limited liability, if you are a member of the board of directors of a limited liability company.

Part of the chapter has been concerned with the more awkward personal aspects of committee membership, raising difficult issues, asking questions and disagreeing with what is going on. While these are important functions of a committee member (although it must not be forgotten that mostly we are there to do positive work together) they are often best carried out through informal as well as formal structures. So I have stressed making informal approaches and gaining support before plunging into formal committee with difficult issues.

EXERCISES FOR CHAPTER 11

1   Reviewing committee membership
A   List all the organisations in which you (or the team or organisation) have membership, and sub-committees associated with the main committees. If you are part of a large organisation, you may need to cover internal as well as external committees. Include informal but identifiable groups.
B   In the case of each organisation, list the chair, secretary, treasurer and any other formal officer; then list important people and the roles that they play in the power structure of the committee.
C   List the important issues dealt with by the committee during the past year, and the outcome in each case. Assess whether the outcome was positive, negative or neutral for your own organisation.
D   Following up on C, review whether the work done by the committee and its value to your organisation justified your input during that period.
E   Work out a plan of action for withdrawing from unhelpful committees, or improving their functioning for your benefit.

2   Practising committee work
A   Identify the main committee roles which you (personally) have not undertaken, and where you would like to develop skills. In a team, share this information.
B   In a team, find ways to practice the roles in internal meetings and activities, or by helping team members to take them up in outside organisations.
C   For individuals and team members, review the work of the holders of roles in committees of which you are a member, and make a brief written assessment of how they contributed to each main issue dealt with.
D   Take a committee meeting, keep notes and review the way in which each person carried out their role during the meeting. In each case, decide how you would have undertaken the role, and whether this was likely to be more effective or less effective than the present holder and why.

3   Raising difficult issues
A   For a committee of which you are a member, identify a difficult issue which you want to raise.

B   Write a brief account or make a verbal statement of your plan of action for raising the issue.

C   Review your plan with another colleague or with your team.

D   Role play any crucial meetings or contacts in your plan.

Twelve:
committee and meetings strategy

WHY YOU NEED A STRATEGY

Joining a committee, or meeting to link your organisation with another or to gain benefits for people you are concerned with is not just a matter of going along. To avoid wasting time, and to have the strongest effect, it is useful to have a strategy. It may be worth devising this strategy before a link to a committee or meeting is appointed, because who will go may depend on the intended strategy. The roles discussed here are more complex interpretations of those reviewed in Chapter 10, and you may find it useful to see how these committee roles have developed from the more formal representative roles.

WATCHING BRIEF

Taking a watching brief is acting as an 'observer' who limits their involvement to matters which affect the interests of the people or organisation that they represent. The advantage of this is that you can keep in contact and have an influence where matters which particularly concern you arise, but you do not have to spend the time involved in frequent meetings. More to the point, you can avoid having to get involved in activities not relevant to you, but which anyone who is a regular participant in an organisation must contribute to. A watching brief enables you to stand a bit outside the target organisation. Of course, sometimes this is a requirement, because an organisation will not let you get involved, but you need to keep an eye on what it is doing.

You can do this directly by asking to have specific matters drawn to your attention and promising to take action if necessary. This might not work, of course, due to inefficiency, or because people forget, or because it is not in the interests of the target organisation for you to know when your issues come up.

So a watching brief also means looking at agendas, decisions of committees and any papers you receive to see if matters of concern to you arise. Being part of a network of contacts, so that others will alert you to matters of interest, and keeping an eye on relevant public events and newspapers or journals may also give you a clue about what is going on. If you are entitled to do so (sometimes keeping a watching brief involves working on the outside of a hostile or uninterested organisation) is it also wise to attend a proportion of meetings and activities both to find out what is going on behind the documents and also to build relationships which will help you to intervene later if you need to.

The most important actions to take when keeping a watching brief are, first, to inform yourself fully in the beginning about the target organisation, its structures and activities. Then, a lively and interested contribution to the meetings and visits that you do undertake (even if these are few) means that insiders will feel comfortable about approaching you or contacting you, and will be more accepting of your intervention, because they are more likely to accept your commitment, even if this is from afar.

Ensuring that you receive and read any necessary papers and information helps you to learn about changes as they happen. Responding in writing to requests for information is helpful, again because it raises the feeling among insiders that you are interested, even if you have insufficient time to get actively involved.

One example of my involvement in this role was when working for a mental health charity. I was asked to represent it on the committee of another charity. I did not have enough time to attend regularly or take part actively, but the contact was felt to be helpful to both sides. The Director of the other organisation would ring me up occasionally to tell me about things that he thought would be of interest to my organisation, and once or twice asked me to come to a meeting where they were to discuss a project that might have been of interest to my organisation.

DISINTERESTED COMMENTATOR

In this strategy, you take the line that you are there as an outsider to advise, comment on and influence the work of the people who form the leadership group of the target organisation. Sometimes, organisations recruit people to committees or invite them to meetings with the aim of getting this sort of help. So, going to consultative, review, or inaugural meetings can be particularly influential because that is when organisations are actively seeking to be influenced.

The disinterested commentator role is often appropriate where you are participating as an expert, or where you are asked to help an organisation without taking a direct role within it. Self-help groups often ask a professional to take on such a job.

Disinterested commentary is also a useful strategy where you are opposed to the leadership group. Being evidently disinterested can mean to insiders that you are not intending to be a threat to their position, as they might think if you took a very active opposing line. If others' views are well-entrenched, you may gain more using a disinterested than an active strategy.

Being a disinterested commentator means identifying important issues which arise in the work of the target organisation. Again you should keep a close watch on papers and other materials that you receive or discover. Unlike activity in the watching brief, however, the commentator identifies arguments for and against the various issues and seeks to ensure that they are brought out and taken into account by the target organisation.

It may be useful, particularly if you are attending a meeting, to prepare for any questions that might arise so that you can respond fluently and authoritatively. In this way your advice gathers respect because it is unprejudiced, unbiased and well-informed. As a result, opposing arguments may have their effect when they might not have been raised at all. Where they are strong and insiders have no strong commitment to any alternative, your opposing ideas may even carry the day.

I took this role frequently when I was director of a council for voluntary service. Smaller organisations often wanted my experience of fund-raising, committee organisation and staff management. I would attend meetings and comment on work, often using my experience of social services agencies as well. I was sometimes asked to join the appointment committees for senior staff.

RESPONDENT

Respondents are prepared to be actively involved in a target organisation or meeting, but only on request. It is a useful approach when the respondent has skills or particular interests or where you or your own organisation want to work on particular aspects of the target organisation which you can identify and explain in advance. Whether the use of a respondent works often depends on the acceptability of this approach to the target organisation.

The advantages of this approach over the watching brief or disinterested commentator is that, to the target organisation, you seem much more active and positive. Being actively involved also gives you a better chance of influencing the outcome of your work.

Although I was a formal member and went to most meetings of a medium-sized arts organisation, I took very little active part until there was a need to have a formal evaluation of its work for several state funders, and I was asked to chair this as an involved and committed member, who was relatively independent of the management and work programmes. This respondent role was useful for the organisation, and the continued contact kept me in touch with trends in the community arts field.

ACTIVE INVOLVEMENT

A more positive strategy still is active involvement. This means deciding to play a part in all or most of the target organisation's work, or in the meeting. Not only discussion or debate within meetings, but taking on work outside them may be required. It means that you will have to have capacity and skills which enable you to take on at least some aspects of the work of the target organisation. It enables you to be more aware of and influential on all its work.

Taking up this position is relatively easy. In most organisations and meetings, there is a shortage of people prepared and able to take on work. An active preparedness to do so will lead you quickly to a good deal of influence, partly because anyone who wants to challenge what you do and say will have to be prepared to take on the work, and they are often loath to do so.

One national committee I became involved in for several years is an example of active involvement. I attended almost every meeting, and went to many public and training events, carrying out many minor tasks for the organisation and sitting on a very active staffing and general purposes committee. They were particularly keen to have a representative of councils for voluntary service and equally to have an academic when I changed jobs. For my part, my aim in being active was to promote links with regional, particularly northern, organisations, which the target organisation was weak in developing.

DIRECTED INVOLVEMENT

This form of active involvement includes commitment to implementing particular policies or directions in the target organisation, while not being prepared to work across the whole field of interests of the organisation. Thus, you become actively involved, but with defined objects in view.

Directed involvement allows you to work just on the aspect of a target organisation or the part of a meeting which is relevant to your own organisation or your own needs, without getting sidetracked by other aspects of an organisation or meeting.

Not only may this be efficient in the use of your time, but there are other gains in strategic terms. In most meetings and organisations, there is only so much that any one person can do. We tend to lose credibility if we get over-involved, because other people start to resent the influence we gain. Also, we may not have the expertise to cover a wide range of things, and our failures begin to raise doubts about whether we can be successful where it matters. People just get tired of the sound of our voice always piping up. So, directed involvement can be a very effective way of husbanding our resources to be very active in a meeting or organisation, but only in one part of it.

Another organisation on whose committee I was active was a large representative advisory committee for a substantial government funder. Staff needed considerable advice, and I concentrated on helping with social services voluntary groups, where I had many contacts and much experience, leaving other colleagues to help with other sectors. In this way, I was able to take on a good deal of detailed work, visiting with staff and advising organisations on how to apply for funds, which would have been impossible if I had spread myself more thinly. As a result of the work, I gained considerable influence on staff decisions, and acquired a lot of information which helped organisations apply more effectively for funds.

LEADERSHIP

One of the effective ways of gaining influence in an organisation or meeting is to take up a leadership role. In many groups and meetings, it is quite hard to find a chair, secretary or treasurer, or a chair of sub-committees or working parties. If you are willing and able to undertake these roles, you can create changes very quickly, and also have access to a lot of useful information. This can be a very useful strategy to gain particular ends within a target organisation or in a meeting.

However, it is important not to undertake these roles half-heartedly. Even though you were originally nominated by your own organisation, or went to a meeting to pursue your own interests or those of someone you are caring for, once you take on leadership positions in the target organisation you are morally and practically bound to place its needs before your own. Morally, once you take on an office in an organisation or meeting, you become a representative of that organisation or meeting and not your own person, so you must act on behalf of the collective. Practically, you will not have influence unless you are patently committed to the needs of the group as a whole in a meeting or organisation.

Acquiring a leadership position often means being prepared to take on tasks - often mundane ones - and fulfil them effectively. It is wise, particularly if there may be suspicion of you as an outsider, not to push too hard for power, since this is sometimes resented by others and leads to eventual loss of influence over potential splinter groups. It is better to work hard and cultivate positive relationships with a variety of different interests within the target organisation.

In one organisation of which I am currently a member, I have taken on the role of treasurer, a burden that frankly I could do without, but the organisation which has only recently been set up needed someone to do this crucial job, and I have some ideas for policy directions in its field. Taking up the office will mean a heavier involvement in the organisation's decisions than I could have if I were an occasional member.

CONCLUSION

In this chapter, I have suggested the importance of being clear about the strategy that you should take up when working over a period with a committee or a meeting. This makes the role you want and can accept clearer to the target organisation, focuses your attentions and is a useful basis for managing the time spent on representative tasks.

EXERCISES FOR CHAPTER 12

1   Evaluating committee strategy

A   List each committee on which you are represented.

B   In each case, identify the strategy being adopted currently; if there is no formal strategy, assess current behaviour and decide what strategy is being used.

C   If there are elements of more than one of these strategies at any one time, consider whether these should be allocated to different people and whether your position is clear with the other organisation.

D   List three reasons for the appropriateness of the strategy being used.

E   Evaluate whether the strategy being used is appropriate and whether another strategy would be better.

2   Practising committee strategy

A   Identify any new strategies being used in a committee, or new committees on which you have representation (with the strategy to be used).

B   Role play making your approach to the committee or organisation concerned and explaining your role (to help you practise, the other person should role play not understanding or being obstructive and wanting you to play another role).

C   Identify any roles in which you are uncertain and role play a meeting in which you would carry out that role; alternatively, review how you would apply that strategy to that particular organisation.

Thirteen: reporting back

THE IMPORTANCE OF REPORTING BACK

When you are representing an organisation or individual elsewhere, you usually have to refer back to the constituency - the organisation or person that you came from - whose authority or interests you represent. The arrangements for reporting back need to be planned and set up at the same time as the representation starts.

The reasons for reporting back are:

- to convey information to others about what is happening;
- to convey other information useful to your constituency;
- to get advice, guidance or support in deciding how to act or in taking action;
- to be accountable through some process to the organisation you represent.

METHODS OF REPORTING BACK

Reporting back can be verbal and informal, through a personal talk with key people as seems necessary. Of course, this is the usual way when you are working on behalf of an individual. Generally, however, some formal systems are needed, such as:

- a regular cycle of reports at committee or other meetings;
- a written report at agreed intervals;
- passing on or copying relevant papers to people who are likely to be concerned with them;
- writing a newsletter or a contribution to one.

An important part of reporting back is to make your feedback interesting and entertaining, because this increases people's motivation to listen and respond.

Simply passing on information is not enough. Your organisation has to have a system for ensuring that the information is used and responded to. This should include mechanisms for representatives to raise issues which concern them and for others to raise questions and comments; for meetings or other contacts to be called when required; and for instructions and advice for the representative to be generated and given official backing when required.

Within your organisation, it can also be useful to identify the right people to receive information and make sure that it gets to them directly. Similarly, an agreement with them about how they will react to information provided to them can be helpful. For one thing, this provides feedback to the representative, so that they can be sure that someone is taking an interest in what they are doing, or that all they are doing does not get lost. Equally, your organisation has an interest in making sure that what you do is targeted on the people who can really use it.

It may also be important for your organisation to decide to take some action (e.g. on hearing about a new grant programme from a representative, it must start the process of making an application).

It is sometimes particularly difficult to recognise a threat or a problem, because such things are often wrapped up in a sequence of events and it is hard to decide where the line should be drawn. For example, a social services representative on a voluntary organisation's committee might come to feel that control of the finances are getting out of hand. This sort of feeling often arises out of a sequence of events, in which minor worries or anxieties accumulate. Then it becomes hard to identify the precise origin of the problems. This is where aims and objectives are important. The representative needs to be constantly asking themselves 'why am I here?' and this should help identify events which are crucially relevant to those aims and draw attention to them. Once in this position, it may be necessary to go back over quite a period, looking at everything that happened in relation to finance and make a dossier of information about events. Again, this can help identify where the concerns come from. It may be helpful to go through events with a colleague who can help by testing out your account of events.

It is important not to feed back everything, but to select particular issues and target the feedback to the people who need to know. This can be done even where particular individuals do not receive their own specialised information. For example, in a local committee representing voluntary youth organisations, the person reporting back from the Education Committee of the local authority made notes such as 'this point is important for uniformed organisations' and 'this is a policy change which will affect us all.' Much the same can be done in signposting written reports with explicit sub-headings about the contents of the paragraphs that follow.

MEETINGS: AN EXAMPLE OF REPORTING BACK PROCESSES

One of the most difficult reporting back tasks is describing meetings, which often seem to be very hard to analyse and difficult to explain in an interesting way. Examining this issue in detail also provides an example of how to go about reporting back other events.

The first thing is to consider what the meeting meant:

- in itself;
- for you in your role as representative;
- for the people you will be reporting to.

Many meetings are largely uneventful and sometimes it is hard to see that they have any 'meaning.' But even the routineness of a meeting is a factor: is the target organisation progressing steadily, or in a slack period, or stuck? The theme of the report then becomes an attempt to convey and understand what is important about the target organisation. Usually, however, there are one or two items which took up most of the time and effort at a meeting, and these become the significant things to report back on. Some members of your audience will have interests in some of the minor matters, and it is important not to forget to convey these, either in the full report, or directly to them person concerned.

The representative's role and activity in the meeting is also relevant in the report back. What contribution did you make? Were you trying to get the target organisation to take a particular line, or to prevent them from doing something, or to collect information for your own organisation? Your own group put you there to represent their interests, so they should want to hear what you have been doing on their behalf.

Finally, of course, it is necessary to consider the points which the members of your group need or want to know about, and make sure these are included.

Having arrived at an understanding of the meeting you are reporting about, the next stage is to consider the form of the report. First, do you need to report on the decisions only, or do you need to describe the discussion which led to the decisions? Often, it is only the results of a debate that your organisation is interested in, so the decisions are the main things. You can then describe, for each topic you cover, the issue, the decision and perhaps the main reasons for it.

Sometimes, however, the discussion is also useful. Where there is interest in the process by which a decision was made, or in personalities (e.g. who was on which side), or what points were made and which missed out, you may have to describe the discussion at length. This is often the case when you are reporting on local authority proceedings where political interplay is important. It can also be relevant where further lobbying or campaigning is a possibility. The report will then give clues about which people to approach, presenting their attitudes and lines which might be taken with different people.

Often, people give reports in narrative form; they describe what happened in the order in which it occurred. This can mean that people 'turn off' before they get to the parts that interest them, and a report divided into topics can be more helpful. On the other hand, people can get interested in the 'story' and miss the crucial point about the decision made, or the meaning for your own organisation of what happened. It is worth thinking carefully, then, to see whether, if you must give a narrative, you can draw attention to issues before describing events. You can say something like 'in the next part of the meeting, the issue of X came to the fore...' so that people's attention is concentrated on the crucial point.

CONCLUSION

The purpose of this chapter has been to reinforce the importance of reporting back to the people on whose behalf you are working when you are undertaking representative activities. Thinking about reporting back reminds you of your constituency and their interests, so that you can focus on their interests all the time you are working for them. Reporting back also gives focus to your understanding of the activities in which you are involved. Above all, reporting back is an essential part of effective representation. We are not there only for our own benefit, but for others, and reporting back respects and confirms their interest.

EXERCISES FOR CHAPTER 13

1 Reviewing reporting back arrangements

A List the organisations with which you have linking or representative functions.

B For each contact, list the appropriate people or organisations for a report back, and identify the aims of each report back. Analyse the aims according to the list set out in this chapter.

C For each reporting relationship, list the present method of reporting back, and assess its effectiveness.

D Decide on a reporting back arrangement for organisations or individuals where reporting back arrangements are inadequate or non-existent.

2 Reporting back techniques

A Identify a recent event in a representative arrangement that you would want to report back.

B Write or perform a report back on this event for each of the methods identified in the chapter:
- verbal report at committee
- a written report
- a list of documents which would inform people and an appropriate circulation list
- an item suitable for a newsletter, and an appropriate newsletter to use.

Fourteen:
lobbying

WHAT IS LOBBYING?

The final two chapters of this book move on from representative activities to attempts to apply pressure or influence on behalf of an organisation or individual. Lobbying is applying influence to another person or organisation, outside formal decision-making structures, to get what you want. Influence is pressure; it is anything which tends to induce a change in your favour. 'Lobbying' comes from a political context - it is something done by people seeking to influence political decision-making. By extension, however, it has come to be used about influence-seeking whether in a political context or not. Any efforts to change or develop a policy in another organisation, or change another person's mind is lobbying, but generally the term can only be applied to consistent, planned and organised pressure, and applied to someone from the outside of the decision-making process. You are not really lobbying if your argument with the other person or organisation is a bit desultory. 'Lobbying' cannot really be applied to joint decision-making in your own team or organisation, but it might be applicable to efforts to change a person's mind or the policy of a group within your team or organisation.

Lobbying as a formal organised activity is often carried out by caring people and staff in community services to get policy change of benefit to the people for whom they are caring.

LOBBYING LOCATIONS

Lobbying can be carried out in all sorts of places. As a member of a committee, representatives will often, as we have seen, approach other members outside meetings, to make suggestions or test out ideas before raising them formally.

Lobbying can also be carried out as a formal process. A meeting is requested with the person or group to be influenced, and a case put to them. This is often done with members of political parties or members or staff of decision-making bodies.

Informal lobbying also takes place. The opportunity to meet at social events, on the bus, in the pub, or at events not strictly relevant to the organisations involved often provide a place to mention concerns and seek opinions. Whether formal or informal, then, all these attempts to influence are lobbying.

MEANS OF INFLUENCE

Among the many forms of influence are:

- personal relationships and liking;
- evidence and argument;
- the manipulation of interest and advantage;
- the manipulation of emotions.

Personal relationships

It is more pleasant to agree than disagree with someone who is a friend or constant contact or someone whom you like, and it is normally more difficult to disagree than to go along with them. Forming friendly relationships with people whom you want to influence, getting them to like you and getting to like them yourself not only makes life proceed more pleasantly; it also makes it easier to influence these people into your way of thinking or to prevent them from acting contrary to your interests.

Taking up opportunities for social contact (e.g. going to organised social events, informal social activities, clubs) often helps in lobbying. It will keep you better informed, achieve warnings of impending problems, friendly words in the ear and chances to talk over problems in advance. More generally, it lets others know that you are someone who is around and may be involved in things that they are doing.

An organisation should plan to involve its members in contacts which would permit this kind of lobbying.

Evidence and argument

Influencing people often means presenting them with information that they do not have and presenting arguments in practical terms which explain what you seek and why, or what they should do about it. This is further explored in Chapter 15 on formal presentations. Such material can also be presented informally, as part of conversations on informal occasions, but needs exactly the same preparation and rehearsal as formal argument, otherwise you may not make fully all the points that you want to. I find it useful to think out the sort of points I want to make and the people I want to see, and then rehearse putting the information succinctly and appropriately, before going off to make contact.

It is worth considering who is the right person to make such presentations. I was once summoned to justify a grant received by my organisation for information purposes which the council concerned thought was being used for excessively radical purposes. Our representatives at the meeting were a barrister and solicitor who were members of the committee and could assure the council with unimpeachable probity that they would never consider doing anything illegal or inappropriate. It was very hard for the politicians to attack their arguments, considering who they were; they also had substantial skills as advocates.

Interest and advantage

Britain is not a place where bribery is either common or usually advantageous, because it is so unacceptable in public life that it backfires when it is revealed. However, much argument and debate relies to some extent on recognising shared and mutual interests, or on meeting the needs of the other party without damaging your own interests. Manipulating interest and advantage, then, is a routine part of trying to gain influence with others; we often say, in effect, 'it will be to your advantage to do this.'

In practice, it is often possible to get someone to see that they will lose something if they do not co-operate, or gain something if they do. Such possibilities are part of every negotiation to persuade people to do things that you want but, looked at in another way, may be not far short of bribery or blackmail. It is useful, therefore, to watch out for such pressures. Organisations can look at their activities, funding and political support to see where they might be vulnerable to pressure. An organisation or individual that you are seeking to influence can also be assessed to see whether they are vulnerable.

The things to look out for are funding which depends on supporting a particular policy or political line, threats to lose funding or support, the possibility of suggesting that if we co-operate over one thing we might be helped in another or if we are obstructive in one thing, we might lose advantages in another.

The usual way of dealing with such things is subtle. Someone will draw attention to advantages and risks of what you are proposing, and leave (or perhaps lead) you to draw your own conclusions. Faced with this, it is easy to feel that failing to come into line will be more disastrous than it is. Therefore, a fairly careful assessment is needed of the power of the other party actually to carry out what they imply, and what ways you might have of avoiding or circumventing them. You need to assess these matters against the importance to you or your organisation in doing whatever you propose.

Similarly, if you are going to use this sort of pressure, you should make sure that your threats or promises are credible and capable of being carried out. This is also true of any offers of advantage that you make as part of an ordinary negotiation. If you say 'we will help you with this, if you will help us with that' you must make sure that you can deliver your promises.

Emotions

Under this heading fall the various forms of influence which appeal to the other person's feelings. One possible emotion is their care and concern for the plight of the individual or group you are arguing for. Here, you must be careful that the action you are seeking is the only or best logical outcome from that concern. Most people, even politicians or otherwise powerful people, are caring and are swayed by such arguments, but I have seen a politician moved by arguments put forward, and their mind immediately moved on to the tack of providing the service through the local authority instead of through the voluntary organisation which was putting up the argument and which relied on a grant for the service to sustain itself.

Alternatively, shame or perhaps risk of bad publicity if the other party fails to act may have some effect. Generally, such things can be easily overcome, and positive emotions are often more effective. Shared ideals for public or community service, shared objectives or idealism for a better future can act as a stronger influence on people, and are harder to argue against.

THE LOBBYING PROCESS

Lobbying falls into four phases. First, it is necessary to identify the people or organisations that have the power to get what you want. Look for indirect leverage on outcome as well as direct influence. For example, some Labour-controlled local authorities are susceptible to influence from trade union sources; some

Conservative authorities from business sources.

A good strategy is also to get the same point of view coming from several different sources, and in particular to gain the support of senior officials who may influence politicians, or gain political support if it is officers that you wish to convince. On an education matter, for instance, pressure from teaching staff, administrators, boards of governors and parent associations might be co-ordinated.

The next phase is looking for and planning locations. Then you must collect the arguments, evidence and various other forms of pressure that you might use and judge best how to use them .

Finally, there is the process of deciding which of the people available to you can best approach the people you need to contact, and the ways in which they are going to do it.

At the end of the process, it is useful to get reports from everyone who was involved. These might cover reactions from others to the things that were said and done, arguments and obstructions put up against you, resources used and sources of support. Such results can help you in further campaigns on the same or related subjects.

CONCLUSION

Effective influence outside your own circle is an essential part of work in the social and community services. Organised lobbying requires careful attention to deciding on the right people to influence, and finding the right place, time and resources to undertake it. In this, it is a typical example of many of the aspects of linking work that we have examined in this book. Careful planning and strategy, use of many different settings to gain influence and understanding and empathetic use of interpersonal skills to make the right approaches at the right time are the characteristics of all linking work.

EXERCISES FOR CHAPTER 14

1 Assessing lobbying needs and opportunities

A Identify a list of issues in which it would be useful to you (or your team or organisation) to achieve a change of policy or view in another individual, team or organisation.

B For each issue, identify possible means of influence under each of the four headings given in this chapter.

C Devise a strategy for influence, going through the steps of the lobbying process described in this chapter.

2 Assessing your vulnerability

A Identify a list of issues which are central to your policy or views on the work that you undertake.

B Establish which of the issues you would not be prepared to change, and which would be open to change.

C Considering each 'unchangeable' item first, assess the vulnerability of your organisation to each of the possible means of influence given in this chapter, including likely sources of influence, the means that those attempting to influence you might use, the susceptibility of you, your personnel or your organisation to that influence and ways of resisting these influences.

D Considering 'changeable' items, assess what matters would cause you to change your policy or views, and what influences you would resist. List likely sources of influence and means of resisting them.

Fifteen:
formal presentations

THE PROBLEMS OF PRESENTING YOUR ORGANISATION OR NEEDS

Sometimes, as we have seen, an organisation or the interests of an individual have to be represented in a public forum where either the whole work of an organisation or an aspect of it, or the needs of an individual must be presented in a planned way. This, may mean giving information to a large undifferentiated group as an audience, such as a public meeting, or to a relatively restricted group, such as a committee or even a court or enquiry hearing. Many people who are called upon to do this find it difficult and even unpleasant, because it means putting yourself forward to strangers, often in a formal public setting, as the image of your organisation, or as being the person whose needs you are representing. Careful preparation, however, can make the task easier.

The problematic aspects of formal presentations are given below:

- Their formality and the unease that this sometimes creates.
- The need to give a comprehensive picture, with the consequent problem of squeezing a quart into a pint pot.
- The need to be fair about the organisation or about someone's needs in public, which may compromise or clash with your own views.
- The assumption that you have to be fairly neutral in what you say; this may be less important where you are representing an individual, but, even here, you may want to avoid over-emotional presentations.
- Dealing with an audience that might not be receptive, or may be actively hostile, so that there is the daunting problem of engaging their interest or combating hostile responses.

Four types of formal presentation are common:

- public speaking (whether to large audiences or restricted groups - many of the principles are the same);
- dealing with reporters;
- exhibitions and displays;
- publications.

PUBLIC PRESENTATIONS

Linking personnel are often asked to give formal speeches or presentations about their work or of a case on behalf of their organisation, either to professional audiences or lay people. The aim of doing so is usually to gain:

- support;
- finance or other resources;
- improvements in co-operation and liaison through better understanding of your work or needs;
- advantages for your work by educating others.

Speaking to even quite small audiences requires careful preparation so that you know exactly what you want to achieve and have the resources available to you to do so. Ideally, you should also be prepared to be flexible, so that you can respond to the 'feel' of a meeting; this will mean that you have fewer problems with your presentation and more influence over the outcome of the meeting.

The first stage of *preparation* comes with the request to speak or make a presentation. You need to find out, or work out, exactly what the topic will be, or what you will have to achieve by the presentation. Sometimes you have a choice or some influence on the topic and how it will be presented, sometimes not. Where you have some say, it is sensible to pick a topic or a slant on it which you feel confident in presenting and for which you are in command of the material, so that you will have some flexibility over the content and style of presentation.

Another thing to find out about is the audience. What size will it be, what sex, what age, what state of knowledge, what interest, what previous involvement? This may be particularly important when you are presenting material to a group which will make a decision affecting you or your organisation.

The context of the presentation is important too. Is it part of a series, either over several weeks and months, or one of several in the same day? If so, what other topics are being covered? What is the scenario? Is it part of a larger meeting or event, such as a dinner? Is it formal or informal? This information will allow you to fit in with the audience's needs and expectations, and other aspects of the event of which you are a part.

Similar information is just as useful if you are making a presentation to a committee. A general speech is not required, but a more analytical and reasoned approach, tailored exactly to the concerns of the group to which you are making the presentation.

The next stage of preparation is *collecting the material* for the presentation. Much of this may be in your mind already, but you may need to collect further information or check and update what you are familiar with. If you are speaking on behalf of an organisation or individual, you will also need to consider what their wishes are about the style and content of your presentation.

Near to the date of the presentation, the basic outline of what you will do can be established, and the *facilities* that you will need can be worked out. A fairly simple talk will not need any audio or visual aids, but you will need to consider whether there are any leaflets or other handouts required. It often helps the memory of an audience to have a brief account of the points made or the principal information conveyed in a leaflet.

Other possible aids include:

- a blackboard (and chalk in several different colours for variety, but make sure they are all visible);
- flip chart (with markers);
- overhead projector slides (sometimes called 'acetates' because they are made of acetate; you can get a roll which is attached to the projector and enables you to write on it, or separate sheets; separate sheets can also have a surrounding frame to make them easier to handle);
- exhibition or display boards, either for use in the talk or as a general display available to the audience before or after the presentation;
- audio tapes (used in excerpts since it can be boring to listen to these for long);
- tape/slide productions (which add to the interest of information conveyed by one or the other medium);
- slides;
- videos;
- films.

If you are at the more sophisticated end of this list, you may be familiar with the necessary equipment, but often a local speaker for a national organisation or a junior member of staff from a local authority may not be accustomed to them. In this case, it is vital to see the material and the equipment and practise with it so that all goes smoothly and you can fit what you say into the material available, or use it selectively. Check whether the place in which you are making the presentation provides adequate facilities, such as power points (take extension cables, spare fuses) and blackout facilities. Be ready to manage if the machinery fails. One of my worst experiences was arriving at a hotel which had twice assured me that all the equipment was present to find that their staff member could not get the video to work and the slide projector was without the cartridge to carry the slides. However obvious it seems, it is worth checking precisely what is available and if it is in working condition.

Having identified the topic, aims and basic outline of your presentation, you need to prepare *speaking notes*. It is possible to write out the whole presentation and read it. This requires a good deal of experience and acting skill to carry off convincingly. Even so, if you cannot improvise and you are forced to speak, in most situations it will be acceptable for a formal speech, such as the speech from the chair to an annual meeting. Having a few points to interpolate, such as practical examples of theoretical points, helps to give a more spontaneous impression.

The best approach is to write out the main points of what you wish to say as a series of headings, either on pieces of paper or on postcards which, because they do not flap around, are less obtrusive. If you write the main points large enough to see them from a distance, you need not look down too much. More detailed points can be written smaller and the notes brought closer if you cannot remember them. Include marks where you will use visual aids or examples as it is easy to forget them. I once sat next to a very skilled speaker, a bishop, on the platform of a vast meeting, and he had one sheet with five points on, but in each case he had the first few words of what he was going to say written out so that he got started on the point, and then could carry on with the flow.

A *rehearsal* in front of a mirror or a sympathetic listener will help to fix the presentation in you mind and reduce the need to rely on notes. It also helps to time the presentation, although it is worth including a few points that you can cut out if you begin to overrun on the day and a few more in case you get through it too quickly. Learning whether you are faster or slower in rehearsal or performance can give you a better clue to the running time if you have some experience.

STRUCTURES FOR SPEAKING

Suitable structures for your presentation are as follows - taken from my training package on *Writing for Publication* (Payne, 1990)

The debate:

Statement
>supporting statements or argument, 1, 2, 3 etc.
>evidence for supporting statements, 1, 2, 3 etc.

Opposing statement
>supports for opposing statement
>evidence for opposing statements

Conclusion
>which is right (or what balance of the opposing positions is right)?

This is good for issues of principle or arguments.

The hierarchy:

>There are X points:
>>point 1 - sub-points a, b, c etc.
>>point 2 - sub-points a, b, c etc.
>>point 3 - sub-points a, b, c etc.
>and so on up to X
>argument about the points
>conclusion

This is good for explaining and elucidating.

The narrative:

>Point 1 leads on to point 2 leads on to point 3 etc.
>draw out significant issues, trends, consistencies, conflicts

This is good for histories, case studies and accounts of projects.

The network:

>There are these five issues:
>>issue 1 is relevant to issues 2 and 3 in ways A and B;
>>issue 2 is connected to 4 and 5 in way C;
>>issue 4 is a factor in how issue 2 came about etc.

This is good for explaining complex ideas, or organisations.

Problem-solving:

This is another useful approach to structuring a presentation. You start with a problem or issue, describe various options for dealing with it showing how, in each case, it meets some or all of the parts of the problem. This can be very involving for the audience, as they go in search of the answer with you, but it is easy to get confused between the options and parts of the problem and sometimes it can be repetitive, as the same points can be made in support of several of the options.

MAKING PRESENTATIONS

When making presentations, the first and absolute prohibition must be on making reference to any problems you have in making the presentation. Do not say you are new to this sort of thing or that you are nervous, because then the audience spend their time looking for signs of it (or thinking you are dishonest because there are no signs of it).

In particular, do not suggest that there are any problems with your visual aids. I recently went to a meeting at which the chair of a residents' association gave a presentation to the local MP and councillors about effects of planning decisions in the area. Her first two or three comments were about how the overhead projector slides had been prepared for her and they were not very good but she hoped they would be useful; then she said that the secretary would be putting them on the projector, and she hoped they would get them all up the right way, but would the audience please bear with her if they got it wrong. All this was distracting and unnecessary; she put herself, the secretary and the slide preparation down and almost willed the audience to feel that the presentation was worthless.

When making presentations, it is also useful to have some ideas for involving the audience and keeping their attention. These come under the headings of style and participatory techniques.

Style involves presenting the material in an interesting manner. Vary the speed at which you talk, the tone of your voice and the nature of the material. Include a humorous touch (perhaps a cynical comment or two - jokes are hard to carry off, and beware of putting other people down). Human interest always attracts, hence starting from a description of a case, human circumstances or the work of a particular individual can draw the audience into greater involvement. Use your hands but don't wave them around. Keep still; don't sway; button your jacket (if any); check that blouse, trousers etc. are done up and hair is unruffled before you start.

Participation is more difficult to handle, especially with a potentially hostile audience, which might react unhelpfully to opportunities to make comments. If people talk or rustle, stop and wait for them ostentatiously. If there are unhelpful interruptions, ask the problem members of the audience to let you finish your points first and then they will have the chance to come back at you. The audience will often be on your side out of courtesy if someone is particularly obnoxious.

If you can involve the audience actively, however, it can be very effective. The rule is to find something that will directly affect the audience and get them thinking about your topic in relation to them. You can ask the audience if they have any relevant experience. 'I wonder how many people here have a relative who is over 65... how many have two... three...four...?' might be a good start to presentation on services for elderly people, for example, because it focuses people's minds on how it might affect them and people close to them. Perhaps a small test can be offered, or you might ask questions: 'Can anyone guess what proportion of people suffer from mental illness at least once in their lives?' You can also tell the audience something about themselves (collectively, never pick out individuals). A quick count, for example, and you can apply the general statistic to their numbers.

For longer sessions, of, say, up to an hour, you can ask people to discuss a topic in pairs and groups and report back, following up with a discussion of different points of view. All these methods get people thinking about what you want to say and doing something, so that your topic will stay more readily with them.

PUBLIC ADDRESS SYSTEMS

At large meetings, you may have to use public address systems, speaking into a microphone or loud-hailer. If possible, it is useful to test before the event what the effects of the system might be, so that you can judge how to use it. The basic rule in most halls is to speak normally, keeping your mouth six to eight inches from the microphone. Do not sway to and fro, or turn to speak to the side, because most microphones used in these settings are directional and you have to speak directly to them. Do not get too close to the microphone or hold it to your lips - it looks anxious and inept. If you have some doubt about whether the sound is reaching the furthest members of the audience, ask, but do not ask frequently; again, this sounds unprofessional.

Occasionally, nowadays, you are given a neck microphone or even a radio microphone. Neck microphones are slung on a necklace round your neck or clipped to your tie, dress or lapel, and a wire from them is plugged into the public address system. It is easy to fall over the wire if you move about and to avoid this it sometimes helps to hold the wire up so that it does not dangle around your feet. Far more troublesome is that it is easy to knock the microphone with your hand or brush it with your clothing; avoid this if possible, because it makes a loud noise. A radio microphone is similar, but avoids problems with the wire because the microphone has an aerial which transmits to a radio receiver in the hall which in turn connects with the loudspeakers.

A common problem with microphones is feedback. You hear a screech which happens when the sound from the loudspeakers is so loud that the microphone picks it up and doubles and redoubles the noise. The usual cure for this is for whoever manages the system to reduce the loudspeaker volume. Sometimes you can help by speaking more quietly or moving away from the microphone.

In many local authority council chambers which you may use for formal meetings, there is a system of individual microphones for each place which are turned on and off as you are called to speak. This relies on an operator noting who is speaking and switching on. More modern systems have a personal switch for you to do this yourself or to indicate that you are about to speak (in which case it is important to remember it). If using the old-fashioned system, ensure that people can hear you if you by rising slowly to your feet and start by saying something inessential until you hear the system come on. This gives the operator time to locate you and switch on.

In the open air, modern public address systems offer a high quality of sound, but it is useful to speak slowly and distinctly. In this case, usually, you have to be fairly close to the microphone. There may even be a windshield into which you fit the lower part of your face. A loudhailer, which is sometimes used in demonstrations and to marshall processions, also requires slow, distinct speech and is usually held close to the mouth.

DEALING WITH REPORTERS

This book specifically excludes press and public relations work, but any organisation is likely to have to deal with reporters from, particularly local, press and media. It is always worth getting to know them and helping them in a positive way as much as possible, inviting them to public events and sending in press releases or reports of things an organisation is doing. If they ask to interview you, check in advance what it is about, so that you can prepare your answers, find documents or information for them, and avoid looking silly by not knowing the relevant facts.

You can ask to speak 'off the record' to help the reporter understand something that you cannot discuss openly, but do not abuse this privilege and do not do it unnecessarily. Ask whether it is acceptable before revealing the information. The most common situation where this is appropriate is where information helps the reporter understand the situation, but cannot be made public, for example where it is about the personal affairs of someone, such as a client or member of staff. Usually speaking 'off the record' is respected, but there is always the risk that anything you say may slip into print. I always follow the policy of only saying things that I am happy to have reported. I also always keep my own notes of what I said, in order to be able to dispute misreporting.

Never say 'no comment', because people think you are trying to hide something. Always explain why you cannot discuss that problem at the moment. If you are contacted with a complaint, always say you will look at it very carefully (see Chapter 7 on When Things Go Wrong).

RADIO AND TELEVISION

Many community groups and professionals are asked to give interviews about their work for radio and television. If these are positive, that is the aim is to put across the work of an organisation, the interviewer will help you put across your message. They will ask leading questions so that you can make the points that both of you have agreed that you want to make. Enquire what they are going to ask about in advance; it helps both you and the interviewer if you have time to think up something good to say. Work out carefully precisely what points you want to make, and practice putting them in a few pithy phrases. Try these out on other people. Generally, the brisker and to the point comments will have the best effect. Dress conventionally, smartly but comfortably for television.

If the interviewing is hostile (e.g. about something that has gone wrong), again prepare well, say what you can on your behalf and shut up. Stay calm and quiet. Ask to be told what they will ask you, but do not assume in this case that you will always be told the truth or all that they will ask. Ask to see their report about you or your organisation before you comment. In an interview with someone who is criticising you, make sure you have the last word, if necessary making clear that you are angry and refuse to accept what is said. If all else fails, a loud 'That's nonsense and he knows it' said as the interviewer is trying to close the interview gives you the final point. If hostile interviewing is likely to be a regular part of your lot, or if you are heading a large or controversial organisation, you really need training in being interviewed on television.

EXHIBITIONS

An exhibition is another form of presentation; the process of creating one is beyond the scope of this book. In most cases, however, exhibitions involve people being present to assist members of the public and this is a situation in which you must interest a complete stranger in your topic in a personal way.

The first requirement is to make provision in the exhibition for the presenter. A display board with pictures alone makes this difficult. Provision for an enquiry desk helps, with perhaps some literature for members of the public to pick up. A little self-test questionnaire ('What volunteering have you done?') or a drawing for children, or a petition to sign, a competition or a practical demonstration can all help to draw people. It also makes it easier for them to ask questions or comment.

If the exhibition is mainly of display boards, it is important not to obstruct them or stand in front of them, because this tends to put people off. Standing to the side, or opposite (thus obstructing someone else's display and moving people in the direction of yours) makes people feel no pressure. To approach them, it is useful to have a leaflet you can hand them. 'Would you like a leaflet to give you more information?' is a good starter because 'What kind of volunteering are you interested in?' follows fairly naturally, and it also gives people an opening to say something to you, and give you clues about how you can interest them further. Ask open questions, that people cannot answer with a 'yes' or 'no'.

It is helpful to have some prepared answers to the likely questions from members of the public. Many people do not like to feel trapped in an exhibition by a long diatribe, and a brief positive response overcomes this. Offers to send them further literature or make an appointment later at the office allow them to take a complicated matter further. If you want to improve your mailing list of interested people, find some way of getting their name and address - offering to send something on often encourages this.

PUBLICATIONS

Many organisations seek to present their organisations through publications. These may be relatively formal (as in annual reports) or informal, through newsletters and posters. They may be regularly published, like newsletters, or occasional, such as a pamphlet or book. It is beyond the scope of this book to examine the detail of publishing, and a useful guide is mentioned in the further reading at the end of this book (Vaughan, 1988). Nowadays, many opportunities are offered quite cheaply by desk-top publishing, and a guide to this is also listed (Worlock, 1988).

The aspect of publishing which is relevant to this book is the planning of content, style and type of publication to achieve the results you want. The aims of publications may be:

- to keep people in touch with one another;
- to inform people about your work or the topics that your organisation covers;
- to influence people in their thinking about your subject matter;
- to entertain and distract them (perhaps making them amenable to the other objectives you have).

The style and content of a publication and its regularity will have to be allied to the particular objectives that you have in mind. Style may include the sort of English used; whether it is relatively formal or informal, uses short or complex terminology and so on. You will also be concerned with illustrations and how they relate to any text. Some publications, such as posters or Christmas cards, may be virtually all pictures; others may be mainly text. Another aspect of style is 'corporate image'. This does not only apply to big companies. Generally, you will want your organisation to become recognisable by its publications, and this means making them look consistent - that is what corporate image means.

Methods of production have been revolutionised in recent years by the availability of cheap computers with word processing and desk-top publishing facilities. Cheap and high quality photocopying has also become widely available, and for many local groups the use of conventional printing through local printers or print shops has become less important. Nonetheless, for a big or prestigious job, conventional printing and professional design will be an important aspect of doing any publishing.

There are also legal responsibilities to be considered. Copyright prevents the copying of already published material without permission, and often community organisations are rather casual about using apposite cartoons or cuttings from newspapers and magazines. You are also subject to the laws of libel, and should be very careful about criticism of individuals.

CONCLUSION

This chapter emphasises the importance, in formal presentation of your organisation, of careful preparation both in content and for the style of what you are going to do. You may have to cope with a lot of different circumstances, many of which may be unexpected, and planning gives you greater confidence that you will be able to overcome any problems that arise. Formal presentations also require a great attention to detail, since you are the focus of attention and people will notice more about you than you will about them. Many of the points made in Chapter 4 on 'First Approaches' are also relevant in formal presentations.

EXERCISES FOR CHAPTER 15

1 Strategies for formal presentations

A List the potential groups, organisations or audiences that you would like to influence or inform on behalf of your organisation or the people you care for.

B For each one, identify events or occasions when you would be able to have some influence on them. Decide on a strategy for getting yourself involved in such events.

C For each event, identify the sort of formal presentation that would be appropriate for it.

2 Practising formal presentations

A Identify one or more formal presentation that you wish to carry out.

B Establish the sort of presentation you intend, and then design the presentation; for example
  • if it is a talk to a meeting, prepare the speaking notes and any audiovisual aids
  • if it is an appearance on radio or television, work out the points you want to cover, and a strategy for getting the coverage
  • if it is an exhibition, draw up a design for it
  • if it is a publication, set out chapter headings and a design.

C Review and evaluate the plans you have made with someone else, to check whether you are having the desired effect.

D If possible, role play the presentation.

Bibliography

Aiken, M., Dewar, R., Di Tomaso, N., Hage, J. and Zeitz, G. (1975) *Coordinating Human Services.* San Francisco: Jossey-Bass.

Bayley, M. (1973) *Mental Handicap and Community Care.* London: Routledge and Kegan Paul.

Bulmer, M. (1987) *The Social Basis of Community Care.* London: Allen and Unwin.

Butler, K., Carr , S. and Sullivan, F. (1988) *Citizen Advocacy: A Powerful Partnership.* London: National Citizen Advocacy.

Clarke, S. (1986) *Seeing It Through: How To Be Effective on a Committee.* London: Bedford Square Press

Davies, B. and Challis, D. (1986) *Matching Needs to Resources in Community Care.* Aldershot: Gower.

Dluhy, M.J. with Kravitz, S.L. (1990) *Building Coalitions in the Human Services.* Newbury Park, Ca: Sage.

Domoney, L. (ed.) (1989) *Directory of Community Social Work Initiatives: England.* London: Practice and Development Exchange, National Institute for Social Work.

Grant, G., Humphreys, S. and McGrath, M. (eds.) (1987) *Community Mental Handicap Teams: Theory and Practice.* Kidderminster: British Institute for Mental Handicap.

Griffiths, R. (1988) *Community Care: An Agenda for Action.* London: HMSO.

Hadley, R. and McGrath, M. (1984) *When Social Services Are Local: The Normanton Experience.* London: Allen and Unwin.

Hadley, R., Dale, P. and Sills, P. (1984) *Decentralising Social Services: A Model for Change.* London: Bedford Square Press.

Janner, G.E. (1989) *Janner on Presentation.* London: Business Books.

Payne, M. (1982) *Working in Teams.* London: Macmillan.

Payne, M. (1986) *Social Care in the Community.* London: Macmillan.

Payne, M. (1990) *Writing for Publication.* London: Whiting & Birch Ltd. This pack is available from Whiting and Birch Ltd, PO Box 872, Forest Hill, London SE23 3HL. Price £7.99 (including p&p).

Peel, M. (1988) *How To Make Meetings Work.* London: Kogan Page.

Rice, A.K. (1965) *Learning for Leadership.* London: Tavistock.

Smale, G., Tuson, G., Cooper, M., Wardle, M. and Crosbie, D. (1988) *Community Social Work: A Paradigm for Change.* London: National Institute for Social Work.

Smale, G. and Bennett, W. (eds.) (1989) *Pictures of Practice: Volume 1: Community Social Work in Scotland.* London: National Institute for Social Work.

Vaughan, J. (1988) *Getting into Print: An Introduction To Publishing.* London: Bedford Square Press.

Wagner Report (1988) *Residential Care: A Positive Choice.* London: HMSO.

Ward, S. (1985) *A-Z of Meetings: How They Work and How To Run Them.* London: Pluto Press.

Warham, J. (1970) *Social Policy in Context.* London: Batsford.

Wilson, D. with Andrews, L. and Frankel, M. (1986) *Citizen Action: Taking Action in Your Community.* London: Longman.

Worlock, P. (1988) *The Desk-top Publishing Book.* London: Heinemann.